The Wells of Salvation

The Wells of Salvation

Meditations on the Prophecy of Isaiah

CHARLES H. and NORMA R. ELLIS

THE BANNER OF TRUTH TRUST

THE BANNER OF TRUTH TRUST
3 Murrayfield Road, Edinburgh EH12 6EL
PO Box 621, Carlisle, Pennsylvania 17013, USA

★

© Charles & Norma Ellis 1985
First published 1985
ISBN 0 85151 457 X

★

Scripture quotations in this publication are from
the Holy Bible, New International Version.
Copyright © 1973, 1978, International Bible Society
Typeset in 11 on 12 pt Linotron Plantin
at The Spartan Press Ltd, Lymington, Hants
Printed and bound in Great Britain by
Hazell Watson & Viney Limited,
Member of the BPCC Group,
Aylesbury, Bucks

Contents

Preface

In 1976, just after we had each read the preliminary
NIV paperback translation of Isaiah, the idea for this
book was conceived. We each felt that in this translation we had been given a glimpse fuller than before of
the beauty of God and his truth. Although we were
devoted to the Authorized Version, we felt that in the
NIV God was speaking to the average reader in our day,
even as he had been speaking to the average person in
Isaiah's day.

This book is the product of many breakfast-time
readings and re-readings, discussions and research, so
that, although the actual authorship is Norma's, the
work is in the deepest sense a joint effort. And as we
have worked together we have prayed that the Lord
would keep us from error and enable us to communicate his truth to our readers. We have prayed that the
Holy Spirit would make us all responsive to his leading
and teaching and enable us together to drink of the
wells of salvation.

If others are as much blessed in the reading as we
have been in the writing of the book we shall be
thankful to God.

Charles and Norma Ellis
Owl's Head, Maine
1984

Wise for Salvation

[*2 Timothy 3:10–17*]

Paul encouraged young Timothy to continue in what he had learned, bearing in mind those from whom he had learned. Who had his teachers been? Paul himself, other elders probably, and before them his mother and grandmother who had taught him the Scriptures.

And what were these Scriptures that were taught him? The New Testament had not yet been compiled, although some of the letters were being circulated. The 'Scriptures' were the Old Testament. And Paul told Timothy that these Scriptures could make him wise for salvation.

Isaiah, perhaps more than any other book of the Old Testament, speaks of salvation clearly and beautifully. It has been called the Gospel according to Isaiah, as it sets forth salvation by the grace of God through faith in his Son. In fact, the very name *Isaiah* means *The Lord of salvation*, that is, *The Lord is the source of salvation*. And Isaiah was described by Jerome as the Evangelical Prophet.

From this book men through the years have been able to draw the waters of salvation, as from a well. And this salvation is not different from that which our children learn today, the salvation of the New Testament. In fact, the book of Isaiah is quoted or referred to more than 210 times in the New Testament. It is regarded as authoritative and it is in complete harmony with New Testament teachings.

Notice that Paul says that the Scriptures, the Old Testament writings, are able to make Timothy wise unto salvation through faith in Jesus Christ. Isaiah, as he sets before us the thrice-holy, sovereign God to whom we owe all we are that is good, also sets forth the Branch who will come from the root of David. In him Israel was to trust . . . and Timothy. In him we must also trust.

Come with us for these weeks to the wells of salvation which Isaiah sets before us. Pray for wisdom to see Christ in the pages of the Old Testament. For God's book is one book with one message. We do not discover the depth and breadth of God's message when we study only part of his book. Each part is placed there to present to us some special facet of the gem, which is the knowledge of salvation.

O Lord, help us, as we read together the Gospel according to Isaiah, to become wise unto salvation through faith in Jesus Christ. Thank you for the depth of the prophet's message. Stretch our minds and hearts to attain to its treasures. Thank you that Christ is there, in whom are hid all the treasures of wisdom.

I Reared Children

[Isaiah 1:1–17]

> *How sharper than a serpent's tooth it is*
> *To have a thankless child!*

So the devastated King Lear cried out. Shakespeare, in these words of a father who, granted, was obsessed with an inordinate desire for affection, still verbalizes the ache that unresponsive children cause a parent who has sought to bring them up with love and care.

The Holy Spirit takes that same experience and uses it to help us penetrate to the heart of the Heavenly Father:

> *I reared children and brought them up,*
> *but they have rebelled against me.*

The children whom God had faithfully nourished did not understand him or know his design for them, though he had patiently dealt with them. They did not show the intelligence or responsiveness of even an ox who knows his master or a donkey who recognizes his owner's manger.

Isaiah describes his contemporaries in Judah, and especially Jerusalem, as sinful, loaded with guilt, evildoers, given to corruption. The most heinous of their sins, that from which the others stem, is rebellion. God had been blessing them with political and economic prosperity during this period, but they had turned their backs upon him. Spurning his holiness they had departed from his ways. They had been thankless children.

God asks why Judah persists in this rebellion. Already she has experienced his discipline. There is no place left on her miserable body which has not felt the rod of his loving correction. Why do God's people, his children, continue to behave in such a way?

Already Judah had known the invasion of the foreigner and experienced the looting and devastation of her land. One day only Jerusalem herself would be left, she whose proud white stones now gleamed in the sun on Mount Zion. She would be like a frail temporary shelter in a garden of cucumbers! But for the grace of God the daughter of Zion would, like Sodom and Gomorrah, be totally destroyed.

What was God's complaint about Judah? Her people were following God's prescriptions, coming to him as he had appointed, but their heart was not in their worship. There was little harmony between their worship and their lives. A holy God cannot allow into his presence a people who are stained with sin. They need first to be cleansed. They need to come into his presence with a humble and repentant heart and a life that conforms to his will.

O Lord, you are now speaking to your rebellious children of the spiritual Israel of the twentieth century A.D. as you once spoke to your children of the eighth century B.C. You hate our worship, too, when our hearts are not in it. You want consistency between our worship on your day and our behavior on all the days of the week. As we read through Isaiah help us to hear your voice and to turn from our rebellious ways. Take us to the wells of salvation where alone we may be cleansed. Bring us to Christ.

Let Us Reason Together

[*Isaiah 1:18–31*]

How often do we say of a child or an adult who has never quite matured, 'You cannot reason with him.' And we give up trying. God had every right to take that stance with Judah. And he has every right to take that stance with us who, like Judah, too often do not respond to him. For we, like Judah, can be duller than barnyard animals.

But our God is gracious. Though rebellion has distorted the thinking of his people, he respects them by appealing to their reason. He, who is the author and essence of reason, as well as of holiness, is willing to sit down with men and present to them a proposition which will make possible the restoration of the spiritual relationship on which his heart is set. He, the personal God, holds out to them as persons a promise of cleansing as they are obedient to him. If, however, they persist in their ways, he warns them that he will be compelled to accomplish their return to him by the sword of an enemy. And, if they reject the pardon he holds out, the blame for their destruction will rest upon themselves.

But how can such a people stop doing wrong? We,

who ourselves struggle with sin, ask this question. How can a city which is forsaking her divine husband for strange gods again earn the name City of Righteousness, the Faithful City? Is it not naïve to expect these people simply to turn over a new leaf and begin doing good works which will win them favor with God? Isaiah is not making such a simplistic suggestion. Their righteousnesses would be filthy rags still. They are responsible for being obedient, but no obedience they can muster will make them clean in the sight of a God whose purity dazzled their fathers at Sinai. Their transformation must be accomplished by God himself. This is the message of Isaiah: God, providing the cleansing waters at his own well.

In perfect harmony with the New Testament, Isaiah portrays a full-orbed gospel. He urges repentance, faith and obedience. These go together – the faith of the penitent heart and the grateful obedience that gives the faith flesh. We see this in his introductory chapter and we see it throughout the book: God provides cleansing water for his people and a cleansed people respond in love by obeying him.

Thank you, Heavenly Father, that you are a personal, reasonable God. Thank you for regarding us as persons, persons able to reason and with whom you are pleased to communicate. May we listen in faith to your gracious words. Renew and transform our minds and lives as we commit ourselves to yourself.

The Mountain of the Lord

[Isaiah 2:1–5]

God had told his people through Isaiah that
Jerusalem would be called The City of Righteousness.
In chapter two the prophet speaks at greater length
about what lies ahead for this city.

Zion was one of the hills upon which Jerusalem, the
capital of Judah, was built. It was the mountain where
God's temple stood. So it became a very special
mountain, at the heart of the city. The word *Zion* came
to be synonymous with Jerusalem and the house of
God. It came to be used for God's people themselves. In
many of our great hymns the terms Zion and Jerusalem
are appropriately used to represent the church. John
Newton's hymn is an example:

> *Glorious things of thee are spoken,*
> *Zion, city of our God.*

God tells Israel that one day 'the mountain of the
Lord's temple' no longer will be part of a harlot city. It
will tower above the mountains of the world. It will be
chief. God's worship will be *the* worship. And the living
and true God of Zion will have his rightful pre-
eminence over the false gods of this world.

As Zion flourishes, the nations around will see and be
amazed and they will stream into it, seeking what it has
to offer. The church of God will open its doors to the

Gentiles who will be saying one to another, 'Come, let us go up to the mountain of the Lord.' Some eight centuries before the Lord was to let down a sheet before Peter and tell him that what God had cleansed no man was to call unclean (Acts 10:9–15), Jehovah here tells his people that the day will come when all nations will stream into his temple.

Why will they come? To be taught God's ways, because from Zion the law of God will go out and the Word of the Lord from Jerusalem. The word of peace and light will shine forth from this mountain and men will see its glory and desire it. They will also regard the Lawgiver and Judge. He will settle disputes and make righteous judgment. Under him the nations will turn from war and hatred and ugliness in their relationships with one another.

This is the vision God held out before Israel. This is the message of the prophet for his contemporaries. They needed such a vision as a day of desolation loomed before them. They needed to have their sights set beyond their times of distress to the day when God would come and dwell among them in the flesh and usher in the gospel age and the eternal kingdom.

We need this vision, too, we who are the church of Christ, Zion, the mountain of the Lord. In times of discouragement we need to be reminded that nations *are* streaming into his church. In every continent there are those who are saying, 'Come, let us go into the house of the Lord.' And as men are experiencing the peace of God they are enabled to settle differences in love.

As men riot in the streets, as they assassinate the heads of state, as the state itself sanctions the killing of unborn children, we allow ourselves to lose faith and be discouraged. We allow ourselves to lose sight of the

[16]

work God is doing in hearts all over the world – a quiet, invisible work, but an eternal work. Satan tries to rob us of the joy we should have in the knowledge that in very truth the earth is being more and more filled with the glory of God as the waters cover the sea. He tries to silence our praise to our Sovereign God for his bringing to pass what he foretold here in Isaiah 2.

And along with the vision of the mountain of the Lord, we, as well as Isaiah's compatriots, sorely need the prophet's exhortation that we should live in accordance with the laws of our Lawgiver and Judge:

> *Come, O house of Jacob,*
> *let us walk in the light of the Lord.*

When He Rises to Shake the Earth

[*Isaiah 2:6–22*]

Men today are being drawn by Eastern religions. Buddhism and Islam are on the upsweep in Western lands. Men practise witchcraft and astrology. Satan has his devotees. God's people blur their distinctives and worship with unbelievers. Our land is wealthy beyond comparison. Isaiah, in describing his own people, was also focusing a telescopic lens upon our contemporaries who have all that money can buy, but are so hungry spiritually that they grasp for husks, even husks held out by the Eastern priests.

Just as the vision of the Faithful City, mentioned

briefly in chapter one of Isaiah, is described more fully in chapter two, so too is the prophecy of the fate of those who forsake the Lord amplified here. Side by side with the description of the glory of God's people stands a description of the humbling of the proud who will not acknowledge their Maker and the destroying of the gods they have fashioned. We shall continue to see these two distinct peoples and God's future plans for them developed throughout the book.

Indeed, idols will totally disappear. Everything that men worship other than the true God will vanish. Men will throw away their idols just as the Ephesian sorcerers of Acts 19:17–19 threw away their scrolls. They will flee to caves in the rocks, seeking to hide from the Holy One of Israel, as their first parents sought to hide from him among the trees in the garden. For the

> *dread of the Lord*
> *and the splendor of his majesty*

will overpower them

> *when he rises to shake the earth.*

Isaiah's prophecies contain many words of warning. And as God through him warns Judah, so he warns our generation to go to the rocks and hide in the ground. Before the splendor of the majesty of God, the arrogance of man will be pulverized along with the gods he has made. Pride, our arch-enemy, will be brought low – pride, that keeps the sinner from bending the knee to God and keeps the saint from making daily confession to his Lord and to his fellows. Like tall trees, high buildings, great ships and fortresses that are brought low, the proud will crumble and the Lord Jesus will be exalted.

[18]

In Hebrews 12:22–29, God takes us to Mount Zion, the heavenly Jerusalem, before his throne around which the company of the redeemed gather. He tells us that if men who would not listen to his warning from Mount Zion did not escape, neither will they escape who do not listen to his warnings from heaven. At Sinai his voice shook the earth; one day his voice will shake not only the earth but the starry skies. Created things that can be shaken will be removed finally, and there will remain only those things which cannot be shaken – heavenly things.

What are we to conclude from this? We are to listen to God *now*. Since, by grace, we are receiving a kingdom that cannot be shaken, we are to be thankful and worship God reverently, aware that he is a consuming fire.

After the Babylonian captivity Israel did turn completely from idols. Today there are men and women who are throwing away their idols, their evil scrolls. As God's Word is preached, east, west, north and south, they are removing the idols from their shelves and from their hearts. As the Holy Spirit renews minds, men are turning from their humanistic philosophies and burning the books upon which their proud thinking has been based. God is shaking the earth even now.

O Lord, if we are clinging to any idols or scrolls, help us to hurl them upon the pyre so we can face you unashamed. Turn us from everything that keeps us from you. Thank you, O Lord, for eternal truths, the unseen things that will never pass away!

They Parade Their Sin

[*Isaiah 2:22–3:12*]

A dear young girl confessed to us that she was not shocked at anything. She and many of her peers are so used to immorality that they accept it calmly and without emotion. They speak casually about their sin and do not attempt to hide it. A periodical captured this in the following quote: 'A few years ago, young women blushed if they were embarrassed. Today, they're embarrassed if they blush.' This sounds like Jeremiah 6:15,

> . . . *they have no shame at all;*
> *they do not even know how to blush.*

And this callousness extends beyond youth.

We who are older are told that human nature does not change; that there was as much sin in the youth of our generation as there is among young people today. It would be difficult to refute that statement. But there *is* a difference. In the days when the laws of God had more credence, there was an attempt to hide sin. It was something of which one was ashamed. Now, when God's law is not regarded, morality has a hollow sound. People parade their sin, not even recognizing it as such. 'Termination of pregnancy' sounds quite innocuous, and why make a fuss over getting rid of a 'product of conception'? As we refer to sin in innocent-sounding terms we come to deny its very existence. Even Dr. Karl Menninger, not a theologian, has been moved to ask, 'Whatever Became of Sin?'

God could not overlook the sins of Judah. Promises of distant glory for Zion and warnings of general calamity for her enemies were not enough to bring back the rebellious children to their father, so here prophecy of a more imminent and specific calamity is provided to jolt the people.

God warns of woes that will begin to come in the lifetime of the readers and will continue even after the Exile. There will be drought and famine in Jerusalem. 'All the officers and fighting men, and all the craftsmen and artisans – a total of ten thousand' will be carried into exile. 'Only the poorest people of the land' will be left (2 Kings 24:14). And in their place will be incompetent leaders, *mere children*, and *women*, as Isaiah calls them. The simple fact that a man wears a cloak, or simlah – the garment of the very poor – will make him a candidate for leadership. But who would want to govern a ruined city and a fallen province, a city and province that had provoked God by their words and deeds? Vividly God pictures a Jerusalem unimaginable at the time of Isaiah's writing. And in this Jerusalem there would be, too, 'a famine of hearing the words of the Lord' (Amos 8:11).

What is in men's unbelieving hearts will be evident on their faces. Like the people of Sodom, men will be brazen about their sin and flaunt it. 'Woe to them! They have brought disaster upon themselves,' Isaiah says of them. Evil pursues the wicked. Leaders, instead of directing the people back to God, will lead them astray from his paths.

We, too, need forgiveness as a nation. We need

sensitivity to sin. We need not only to be shocked at Judah's sins but embarrassed at our own.

O Lord, help your children, who have the advantage over ancient Israel of a completed revelation and who have the abiding Spirit, to be aware that much of the church today, like Isaiah's Jerusalem, staggers. Help us not to parade our sin but to confess it. Help us to stand out against the many and remain righteous, though we be but a remnant.

Then will Isaiah's word rejoice our hearts:

> Tell the righteous it will be well with them,
> for they will enjoy the fruit of their deeds.

In That Day

[*Isaiah 3:13–4:1*]

Turn back to Isaiah 2:12 and see where God tells that he has set *a day* for the humbling of the proud and mighty. And to verse 17 of that chapter where he adds that he alone will be exalted *in that day*. Verse 20 goes on to say that men will cast aside their false beliefs and seek refuge from the Lord *in that day*.

In the present chapter Isaiah describes a time when Zion's women, proud in their demeanor and in their wardrobe, will find their clothing and adornment gone. To 'stretch out the neck' meant to be haughty: the haughty will be brought to shame. Instead of fragrance there will be a revolting stench; instead of a stylish belt, a frayed robe; instead of high fashions, rags; instead of beauty, disfigurement.[1] *In that day* their pride will be exchanged for mourning for their husbands who have died or been carried away into captivity.

The term *in that day* is used by Isaiah some forty times with a variety of meanings. It sometimes forebodes judgment. But as we go on to read we will see its meaning becoming clearer. In general, *that day* begins with the first coming of Christ and extends to his coming again. It embraces the events that are involved with the defeating of Satan by the Lord Jesus. It is the time of the vanquishing of the foes of God and of his people, of judgment visited upon sins by the presence and work of God's Son on earth and the presence and work of his Spirit during the church age. And *that day* extends to the complete victory of the Lord Jesus when history will be wound up at his second advent. Implicit in that victory is the defeat of all his enemies. It looks far ahead of Isaiah, beyond Christ's earthly sojourn and on into eternity. It is a general term and may be regarded as synonymous with *the last days*.

This is not to say that there was nothing in the content of passages referring to *that day* that was prophetic of Israel's history as a nation. The calamities foretold in these passages had proximate or immediate fulfilment in many cases as God's people experienced judgment at his hand for their sin. God permitted foreign powers to humble his people that they might be brought to seek his forgiveness. These passages, which so frequently had overtones of judgment, were very meaningful and purposeful as they came from the lips of the prophet and from his pen. They were dagger thrusts; or, rather, they were surgeon's scalpels, meant

[1] *Branding* was self-inflicted to symbolize grief.

to cleanse the nation from its disease and restore it to soundness and health.

History moves on and the impact of *that day* will be experienced increasingly as the culmination of all things draws near. To us and to our children the future is a glorious hope, with the victory of our Lord and Saviour manifested more and more in the lives of men and women all over the world. We anticipate his coming on the clouds and we sometimes think we hear faint strains of the heavenly chorus in the distance. *That day* is the day of salvation realized.

But *that day*, in its final fulfilment, is also a day of terror. As evil becomes more and more blatant and unrestrained we sometimes feel the foreshadowing of judgment. We sense that the Lord will soon have had enough of man's sin and the curtain will be closed on the tragic enactment of rebellion against man's Maker. *That day* is the time of the final settling of accounts.

That day is now. The Lord Jesus has come with the good news. His Spirit is at work as his servants are occupied spreading his gospel to every tribe and nation. Let us rejoice in what is before us and cling to him, though intervening shadows hang heavy before the light blazes forth in eternal day.

The Branch of the Lord

[*Isaiah 4:2–6*]

Israel's reigning family is often pictured as a tree. The main trunk of this family tree has been cut down and only a stump remains. Then a fragile shoot comes forth which will in that day develop as the Branch of the Lord, beautiful and glorious. In Isaiah 11 we will see this figure of Messiah the Branch expanded. Here the prophet introduces it to us. These verses form a splendid unit that brings to us a picture of the coming of the Lord Jesus.

David had been promised by God that never would the throne depart from his family. With sad eyes we read the history of the kings of Judah and note the decay of the grand old tree, perhaps wondering about God's promise. But in this chapter God reinforces his plan for David's line. Jeremiah also strikes the same note:

The days are coming, declares the Lord,
When I will raise up to David a righteous Branch . . .
(Jeremiah 23:5)

Zechariah takes up the theme:

I am going to bring my servant, the Branch.
(Zechariah 3:8)

Later, in chapter 6, verse 12, this same prophet adds:

. . . This is what the Lord Almighty says: Here is the
man whose name is the Branch, and he will branch out
from his place and build the temple of the Lord . . .

Though centuries passed, the hope that the Branch would come did not disappear. Now hear the people singing on Palm Sunday,

Blessed is the coming kingdom of our father David!
Hosanna in the highest!

See men spreading garments in the way for a red carpet (Mark 11:1–10). The promised king *was* raised up in the line of David. His legal or foster father, Joseph, had David's blood flowing through his veins. His mother, Mary, was also of the line of David. In Jesus the kingdom promised to David forever was established. He said, 'I will build my church.' And as head of his church he reigns in righteous judgment and justice. He is the Branch of Isaiah 4!

So closely intertwined are the king and the kingdom that Isaiah immediately speaks of the survivors of Israel, the remnant, and the fruit of the land which will be their pride and glory. To refuse to see the spiritual and worldwide reference to Zion here is to dwarf God's revelation – and, indeed, to dwarf the Branch himself! The kingdom of the Branch is the church universal. Christians are, in the sight of God, holy, washed by the Lord. Their cleansing is gentle washing with God's waters. But this cleansing is also drastic, with a spirit of judgment and a spirit of fire.

God will protect his people. He will extend a canopy over them, a tent fashioned with love. That canopy will shield them from the scorching sun and from storm and rain. And he will be with them as he was with his people when he guided them through the wilderness with the pillar of cloud and the pillar of fire.

Thank you, O our Lord, for our King – the Branch from the family tree of King David. Thank you for the promise that there will be a day when he will be vindicated. Thank you that we shall be protected eternally in his presence. This will be fulness of joy!

What More Could Have Been Done?

[Isaiah 5:1-17]

Isaiah's song of the vineyard is the song of God himself. It calls to mind the lament of the Lord Jesus as he looked over the city of Jerusalem centuries later. How often would our Lord have gathered the people unto himself as a hen gathers her chickens under her wings, but they would not. The great heart of the Saviour yearned over Jerusalem but they had no regard for his deeds or respect for the work of his hands.

Here in Isaiah is a lament of the Father and the Son over the hardness of men who were called to receive special blessing from God. These people were cared for gently, as the fields of a good farmer are tended. The site was chosen thoughtfully, a fertile hillside with good drainage. It was cultivated and cleared of stones. The choicest sturdy plants were set in. A watchtower was built to provide for detection of possible human or animal marauders. And the winepress was ready for the anticipated harvest.

But instead of the good grapes which the master of the harvest had reason to expect, the yield was bad fruit. Instead of the justice the Lord Almighty expected from his people, there was bloodshed; instead of righteousness, the distressful cries of the oppressed.

What will the master of the vineyard do? He will take away the hedges that protect it, and its walls. The vineyard will become a wasteland, neither pruned nor

[27]

cultivated. Briars and thorns will grow up. The Sovereign of the weather will command the clouds not to rain on it.

What judgment will the divine vineyard-keeper pronounce upon it? A ten-acre vineyard will produce only a few gallons of wine. Six bushels of seed will yield only a half bushel of grain. Lambs will feed among the ruins of the rich man's estate.

Because men have no regard for the deeds of the Lord, no respect for the works of his hands, they will be brought down from their high places. Their lives of leisure and pleasure will be brought to an end. They will go into exile for lack of understanding.

But the Lord of the vineyard will be exalted by his justice and will be shown holy by his righteousness. After he had borne long with them, and they still persisted in their own sinful ways, he cannot be held accountable when judgment has to fall. What more could he have done for them than he has done?

The Lord Jesus told the story of the unfruitful fig tree. The gardener digs around it, cultivates it, prunes it. Patiently he refrains from cutting it down. But the time may come when he can wait for fruit no longer. And when the tree is finally cut down he will be justified (Luke 13:6–9).

The fig tree and the vineyard supply one teaching. And they belong to the farmer or gardener, Christ.

> *I will sing to the one I love*
> *a song about his vineyard:*
> *My loved one had a vineyard*
> *on a fertile hillside.*

With insight and gentleness born of God's Spirit Isaiah saw a picture of his beloved Lord and the people he had

chosen and gave it to us in a tender and poignant
parable.

> *Lord Jesus, you have dealt with us in grace and mercy.
> You came to be one of us. You served. You taught. You
> resisted sin. You suffered. You died. Ours is the
> responsibility to bear fruit, much fruit – for you. We
> cannot do it alone, but if we abide in you as the branch
> abides in the vine, the fruit will come. Help us, we pray.*

Bitter for Sweet . . . Sweet for Bitter

[*Isaiah 5:18–30*]

As people grow older they often lose their sense of
taste. What a blessing it is to have a keen sense of taste
and to be able to enjoy all the subtle differences in flavor
that God has built into the array of delicious foods he
has provided for men!

An inability to distinguish between tastes can overtake our moral and spiritual senses, too. And at any age.
Men who reject the wholeness of God find their
personality becoming fragmented and twisted so that
they confuse good and evil. Their judgment cannot be
trusted. When they taste something sweet they think it
is bitter. The things of the world attract them; the
things of God have no appeal.

The Psalmist invites us: 'Taste and see that the Lord
is good' (Psalm 34:8). When men refuse even to taste
they assume that the ways of the Lord are sour or

uninteresting. So they never get to experience the liberty and sweetness of the heavenly Father or to bear testimony to his grace. They never get to sing,

> *How sweet are your promises to my taste,*
> *sweeter than honey to my mouth! (Psalm 119:103)*

Isaiah cries out woes to those whose rejection of God has brought them into such confusion. He says:

> *Woe to those who call evil good*
> *and good evil,*
> *who put darkness for light*
> *and light for darkness,*
> *who put bitter for sweet*
> *and sweet for bitter.*

Six times in this chapter God pronounces woe upon sinners. Six times in Luke 11 the Lord Jesus declares judgments on the sinners in his day. Here, as there, in gripping metaphor the nature of sin is drawn, and the pile-up of woes and judgments makes a tremendous impact upon the reader. In verse 8 greediness is pictured; in verse 11, pleasure madness; in verse 13, deceit; in verse 20 – upon which we have just focused our attention – distortion of values; in verse 21, pride; and in verse 22, injustice.

Beginning at verse 24 Isaiah categorizes the persons he has just described: they have rejected the law of the Lord Almighty and spurned the word of the Holy One of Israel. Basic to all sin is the rejection of God and his revelation. This is the sin that spawns all other sins. The first commandment is *the* commandment. 'You shall have no other gods before me' means you are to make *God* your God. Or, to shift the emphasis, it means you are to make God your *God* (See Exodus 20:3).

Failure here is the sin of every age. When we act as rebels, and have no desire that God should rule and regulate our lives, we are out of line. We seek to accumulate worldly possessions. We turn to pleasure for fulfilment. Deceit overtakes us. Our values are overturned. Pride blinds us. And there is injustice in our dealings. As Isaiah piles up these six woes, he exposes the way in which a denial of God colors all aspects of our lives.

Woe to those who reject God and his law! Of them Isaiah says,

> *. . . As tongues of fire lick up the straw*
> *and as dry grass sinks down in the flames,*
> *so their roots will decay*
> *and their flowers blow away like dust.*

This Has Touched Your Lips

[*Isaiah 6*]

This is the story of what happened when Isaiah saw the Lord. It is the story of Moses at the burning bush hiding his face at the sight of Jehovah. It is the story of Job prostrate before his God: 'My eyes have seen you. Therefore I despise myself and repent in dust and ashes' (Job 42:5 and 6). It is the story of Peter, calling to Jesus from his boat as it was sinking under the miraculous catch, 'Go away from me, Lord: I am a sinful man' (Luke 5:8). Is it your story and mine?

Isaiah saw the Lord. We read it not only here but in John 12:41 where the apostle, after commenting concerning unbelief in the miracles of Christ, quotes from this very chapter, saying that Isaiah saw the glory of Jesus and spoke about him. Isaiah, like Moses and Job and Peter, had an experience which made him aware to the depths of his soul of the holiness of God. He heard the seraphs singing,

> *Holy, holy, holy is the Lord Almighty:*
> *the whole earth is full of his glory.*

The seraphs required a trinity of *holies* to describe God. And Isaiah was permitted to witness the glory of the Holy One of Israel. In his book he uses this term *Holy One of Israel* twenty-three times, whereas it appears elsewhere in Scripture only a half dozen times. The experience of seeing God was not lost upon him.

The gleaming beauty of God's holiness was like a mirror held up before the prophet. He saw his own filth and need. Notice, it is his lips which he especially perceives as unclean, and the lips of his people. Salt water flowing from a stream belies the existence of fresh water at its source, as James implies in his discourse on the tongue. Our lips give evidence of what is in our hearts; Isaiah clearly perceived the heart of man in himself.

Did the prophet frantically hurry to cleanse himself? No! To confess to God his ruined condition was all he needed to do. God did the cleansing. Symbolically we see this as the seraph takes a coal, which he has lifted from the altar with tongs, and with it touches Isaiah's lips — those lips Isaiah had just called unclean. The touch of the coal symbolizes the redemptive work of God at the altar where our Lord was crucified. It symbolizes here, also, the sanctifying of the lips of the prophet that he might speak the words of God.

Now, humbled and cleansed, Isaiah is ready for commitment. 'Send me,' he pleads with God. And God did send him. His mission was to tell Israel of his vision of the holiness of God and the sinfulness of men. This theme runs all through his prophecy as a fitting backdrop to the gospel drama which he unfolds.

Israel as a nation did not heed Isaiah's words any more than the Jewish nation heeded the words of the Messiah himself, or of Paul, his servant. And God sent his gospel to the Gentiles. It is a message for the whole world.

There are strong and unsettling words in this chapter that shake us, as the sound of the seraphs' voices shook the doorposts and thresholds of the temple. Do they prostrate us before the Holy One of Israel? Do they cause our lips, cleansed by the living coal, to whisper, 'Send me'?

A Virgin . . . with Child

[*Isaiah 7*]

Enemies were coming against the people of God. King Rezin of Syria and Pekah, son of Remaliah, king of Israel, were marching up to fight against Judah. The hearts of King Ahaz and his people were shaken as the trees of the forest are shaken by the wind.

God sent Isaiah to calm the fears of Ahaz and his

people and to assure them that these enemies would themselves soon be too scattered to be a people and to be a threat to them. The head of Damascus, he says, is *only* Rezin and the head of Samaria is *only* Remaliah's son. *Your* head, he implies, is God. He encouraged them in their trust in God:

> *If you do not stand firm in your faith,*
> *you will not stand at all.*

Graciously the Lord gave a sign to his people – a 'virgin will be with child and will give birth to a son and will call him Immanuel.' Before enough time elapses to allow the child to come to the age of discretion, the lands of King Rezin and of Pekah will be laid waste. They will be no threat to Judah.

What will be the instrument of their destruction? Egypt and Assyria! The Lord will whistle for flies from Egypt and bees from Assyria. At his bidding these enemies will devastate the lands of Syria and Ephraim. The armies of the world come and go, rise and fall, at the bidding of the Sovereign Lord.

And if Judah would not repent, these enemies would come even to her. The Lord would use a razor hired from beyond the river Euphrates, the king of Assyria, to shave Judah's head and the hair of the legs and to take off his beard as well.

But what about the sign? The sign of the virgin-born son, Immanuel, was for God's people not only of the days of Ahaz, but for all time. It was a sign to remember through the centuries, as enemies would threaten God's people over and over again, a sign in the face of Satan, the great enemy. The promise of God coming in the flesh was to sustain Judah through the years. It was in him, the King who would conquer all foes, that they must put their trust.

God still brings enemies, working through them his own purposes to humble and refine his people and to bring glory to himself. But he brings deliverance also. His own Son, born of the Virgin Mary, came among men to deliver them from Satan's control. The angel reminded Joseph of the promise when the troubled husband discovered before their marriage had been consummated that Mary was pregnant. The baby's name, Joseph was told, would be *Jesus*, because he would save his people from their sins. He would be born in fulfilment of Isaiah's word to Ahaz, 'The virgin will be with child and will give birth to a son, and they will call him Immanuel' (Matthew 1:23).

For us, too, from where we stand on this side of Bethlehem, the sign of the virgin-born is a cause for rejoicing. Jesus – Saviour! Immanuel – God with us! But the sign of the virgin-born bears the warning from God still:

> *If you do not stand firm in your faith,*
> *you will not stand at all.*

And these words hold good for us, too. Unless you and I are firmly established upon the Son who was promised to Ahaz we will not, cannot stand.

Immanuel

[*Isaiah 8:1–10*]

In chapter 7 we read of a sign that God gave to Ahaz concerning the birth of a child. Here we read of a similar sign. At God's command, Isaiah had intercourse with his wife (she is called the prophetess) and she conceived and bore a son. Before the child was old enough to talk, the prophecy of God was fulfilled: Assyria came and plundered Damascus and Samaria.

Now the Lord speaks to Isaiah again, this time in a remarkable figure. He says that because this people has rejected the Shiloah, he will bring against them the River Euphrates. Shiloah was the stream that originated in Gihon and was channeled later by Hezekiah underground, into the pool of Siloam, which was at that time within the walls of Jerusalem. It was a gentle, life-giving stream. Shiloah means *peace*. Euphrates, on the other hand, means *flood waters*. The Lord is saying that the flood waters of Assyria will sweep over Samaria and Syria and even over Judah, reaching up to the neck. The flood waters (the army of the king of Assyria) will spread out as the wings of a huge bird even over the whole land of Judah. Because the people rejected God's peace they would taste war.

Jesus is our Shiloah, our peace. When he is in the heart there is communion between man and God, peace between brothers in the Lord, and even harmony between our desires and our behavior. To reject Christ is to lay oneself open to the flood waters of sin and destruction from Satan. When we are not resting in the shadow of the wings of the Almighty, the shadow of the Evil One darkens our whole world.

What a delight to meet at the end of verse 8 a kind of prayer, 'O Immanuel!' In chapter 7 we had seen Immanuel identified with the virgin-born One. God's people are directed through the years to anticipate the incarnation of the Lord Jesus who is their rightful King. The judgments foretold here are linked with him. And in the midst of the calamities to come his people may look to him.

God, speaking through Isaiah, now turns from Jerusalem and challenges the enemy nations to raise their war cry, prepare for battle and devise their strategy. With bold irony he challenges them to propose their plans. All of their efforts against God's people will be thwarted, he is saying, because God is with his people.

This refrain, Immanuel, runs throughout the prophecies of the invasion. God's presence is the comfort of his people. They have his promise that, though the flood waters reach up to their necks, he will preserve the righteous. And as his Judah today we have the comfort of his presence, too. The plans of those who would attack us will be thwarted because God is on our side.

Thank you, O Immanuel. Thank you, our Shiloah.

To the Law and to the Testimony

[Isaiah 8:11–22]

Jesus is referred to in Scripture as a rock. Sometimes he is the rock in which his people find sanctuary as birds find sanctuary in a place out of reach of the hunter. Sometimes he is a rock upon which his enemies stumble and fall.

In Isaiah 28:16 we read:

> *See, I lay a stone in Zion,*
> *a tested stone,*
> *a precious cornerstone for a sure foundation;*
> *the one who trusts will never be dismayed.*

Paul in Romans 9:33 refers these words to Christ crucified in whom is our trust. To the called ones Christ is the power and wisdom of God. In him the law and testimony of which Isaiah speaks are comprehended. He has fulfilled the law.

But Christ is also a cause of stumbling and falling, a trap and snare for those who dishonor him. Paul in the same passage quoted verses 14 and 15 (from Isaiah 8) and pointed out that Israel had stumbled over the stumbling block because they pursued righteousness by their own works, not by faith. And in I Peter 2:8 the apostle also quotes Isaiah, commenting that men stumble because they disobey the message.

God's people are distinctive. He does not want them to follow the world – whether that world bows to the heathen gods of the neighboring nations or whether it bows to man himself or the works of his hands. He wants his people to be completely centered in him. They are to pattern their attitudes after his Word. They are not to call conspiracy everything the world calls conspiracy, nor to fear what the world fears. Peter spoke similarly, 'Do not fear what they fear; do not be frightened' (I Peter 3:14). The Lord Almighty is the One his people are to regard as holy, the One they are to fear. This is their distinctiveness.

God's people have an authority different from that of the world. They are not to consult mediums, spiritualists, astrologers. They are not to gather together with other mere men and pool their ignorance without reference to God. Their authority does not rest in men, whether they be learned clergymen, statesmen, scientists, philosophers or psychologists. To the law and to the testimony! Everything that does not issue from the Word of God issues from the darkness of sin and ignorance.

Though God may be hiding his face for a time, Isaiah affirms his purpose to wait for him and place his trust in him. The very names of Isaiah and his sons were given by God to symbolize God's promise of faithfulness. The first of Isaiah's sons mentioned in this context was Shear Jashub, which means *a remnant will return*. The next son was Maher Shalal Hash Baz, which means *quick to the plunder, swift to the spoil*. The name of Isaiah himself may be translated *Jehovah is Lord*. When we read that Isaiah and his sons are signs or symbols to Israel from God, we are to understand that God has been and will be a covenant Lord to his people, always retaining a remnant despite plunder and destruction. Upon this promise Isaiah was standing when he said, 'Here am I, and the children the Lord has given me.'

In Hebrews 2:13 the author applied Isaiah 8:18 to Christ, it is true, and to his spiritual seed. But a double application would not be out of keeping with Scriptural practice.

And surely, as the seed of Christ, we will put our trust in him, and upon him we will take our stand. To his law and testimony we will go. 'For the foolishness of God is wiser than man's wisdom, and the weakness of God is stronger than man's strength' (I Corinthians 1:25).

A Light Has Dawned

[Isaiah 9:1-7]

At the close of chapter 8 Isaiah spoke of men who have no light. Now the prophet-artist splashes against his dark background a breath-taking picture of the Lord of Light. There will be no more gloom, he says, for those in distress; people in darkness will see a great light.

Following his account of the temptation of Jesus, Matthew (4:14) reminds us of this prophecy. Jesus, he says, went to Capernaum, which was in the area of Zebulun and Naphtali, in fulfilment of Isaiah's words. Quoting God's promise that Galilee would be honored, he says:

The people living in darkness
have seen a great light;
on those living in the land of the shadow of death
a light has dawned . . .

Jesus was that light, not only to those in Galilee but in the whole world. This he affirmed when he declared, 'I am the light of the world. Whoever follows me will never walk in darkness, but will have the light of life' (John 8:12).

To the human mind this light, as Isaiah describes him, has irreconcilable components. On the one hand he is a son who will be born, a child who will be given. That light will be a human being. He will be truly man. One who will govern. One in the line of David. But in the same breath Isaiah identifies the light as the Mighty God and the Everlasting Father! He will be truly God. The God the Jews knew as Jehovah. One so holy that his name could not be uttered.

From our vantage point and with an understanding of completed revelation given us by the Holy Spirit, these things, although they are difficult to comprehend, fit beautifully together. But we may well believe that to many Jews in Isaiah's audience the concept of one who was God and man was outrageous. Surely this was true of many Jews at the time of Jesus and it is true today. A few years ago a Rabbi Hertz was quoted as having commented about Isaiah 9:6 in this way: 'This is quite impossible. No true prophet – indeed no true Israelite – would apply a term like "Mighty God" or "Everlasting Father" to any mortal prince.' And indeed, to use the terms of deity with reference to a human being is a concept intolerable to all, unless that being were, in truth, divine as well as human. Paul found it intolerable so he sought to stamp out any who proclaimed it of Jesus. Until the God-man himself appeared to him!

With the coming of the King is the coming of the Kingdom. And how shall this totally desirable kingdom, where justice and righteousness will be bulwarks, be brought into existence? The zeal of the Lord Almighty will accomplish this. It will not be ushered in by man, who from time immemorial has been dreaming up Utopias which have never materialized because of sin (for the only real Utopia is one from which sin has been obliterated). Christ has conquered sin and given his people victory over it. His Kingdom, his Utopia, if you will, materializes as men and women are born anew by his Holy Spirit and given faith to trust and worship the King. Because the Light has come, we in the church today enter into the joys of this kingdom in fellowship with God and his people. One day we shall experience it fully. 'The zeal of the Lord Almighty will accomplish this'.

As we hear the words of the prophet set to the music of Handel we are deeply moved. We know *that the Son who was given is the Light of the world. Help us, dear God, when the strains of the music fade away, not to forget. Help us to live, not as those who are in darkness, but as those upon whom your Light has shined.*

His Hand Is Still Upraised
[*Isaiah 9:8–10:4*]

The hearts of many Christians have been stirred by
the rich, full voice of Ethel Waters as she has sung:

> *He's got you and me in his hands;*
> *He's got you and me in his hands;*
> *He's got you and me, brother, in his hands;*
> *He's got the whole world in his hands.*

These words may have been drawn from Joshua: 'We
are now in your hands. Do to us whatever seems good
and right to you' (Joshua 9:25). God's people are safe in
the hollow of his hand, protected from evil. Since he is
our Sovereign and also our Father, we may rest here in
confidence.

As the figure is changed, we may picture God's hand
upraised in blessing upon us. The Christian experiences peace as he realizes that God's blessing is upon him,
because the judgment due to him was laid upon the
Lamb of God.

When Isaiah was writing the Messiah had not yet
come. The light had not dawned on the land of the
shadow of death. The kingdom of justice and righteousness had not yet been ushered in.

There was pride and arrogance in men's hearts. O
yes, Ephraim and Samaria admit in the first stanza of
this dirge, 'the bricks have fallen down but we will
rebuild with dressed stone'. Yes, the fig trees have been

cut down but we will plant cedars in their place. No humbling of the heart is here, but rather a godless autonomy. And God will strengthen their foes against them. Isaiah closes this stanza with a refrain that pictures God's hand upraised in judgment, not blessing:

> *Yet for all this, his anger is not turned away,*
> *his hand is still upraised.*

Still the people have not returned to the Father who had to discipline them. So the elders and prominent men and the lying prophets will be cut off. The Lord will not take pleasure in the young men or pity the orphans and widows. The whole cross-section of Israel is wicked. And the prophet's refrain runs,

> *Yet for all this, his anger is not turned away.*

Wickedness burns like a fire. All is consumed by it. Wickedness burns, yes, as a tool in God's hand against the wicked. 'For our God is a consuming fire' (Hebrews 12:29). Never will the lust of men be satisfied though they devour each other – or themselves! Again:

> *Yet for all this . . .*
> *his hand is still upraised.*

And the injustice of laws, the oppressiveness of decrees! Where will men go in the day of reckoning? There will be no escape. There will be only a falling among the slain. And a fourth time the awful refrain peals forth:

> *Yet for all this, his anger is not turned away,*
> *and his hand is still upraised.*

Oh, most holy God, sin is ever anathema to you.
Thank you, our Father, that we may experience the
peace of being in your hand. Make us fully aware of our
debt to proclaim the good, liberating news of your Son to
those who are under your judgment.

Wilful Pride . . . the Haughty Look

[Isaiah 10:5–19]

There is a somewhat humorous aspect to pride.
Imagine a tiny poodle barking ferociously at a Great
Dane who stands quietly looking down on him. It is, as
we read in Psalm 2, the kings of the earth who set
themselves and the rulers who take counsel together
against God and his Son, saying,

> *Let us break their chains . . .*
> *and throw off their fetters.*

God laughs as he sits on his throne and watches them.
He holds them in derision. But this is a tragic kind of
humor, a laugh that has a foreboding echo in the
chambers of time.

The Sovereign God sent Assyria to punish a godless
people, to loot and plunder and trample them down as
mud in the streets. Assyria was the sword in the hand of
God to humble a people who angered him, his own
people Israel.

The king of Assyria, however, with wilful pride in his

[45]

own heart and a haughty look in his eye, went about his task, not as an instrument of God to humble the nation and punish it, but as an autonomous power who would utterly destroy it. He claimed to have done everything by the strength of his own hand and his own wisdom. He compared himself to one who reaches into a nest to gather abandoned eggs and meets no resistance, not one hatching chick flapping a wing or opening its mouth to chirp.

In clean, bold metaphor the poet lashes out against the pride of the Assyrian king. Woe to the Assyrian, we read, the rod of my anger! In one rhetorical question after another God asks: Does the axe boast in the face of him who swings it? Does the rod wield the man who lifts it up?

The Lord will punish the Assyrian and his land for this wilful pride. Those who remain will be few like trees in a devastated forest, so few that a child could count them and write down the sum.

Pride is self-destructive. It is self saying to God, *I* not *Thou*. It fails to acknowledge that God is Creator and I am creature. I may be an axe with latent power, but I am only an axe unless God wields me. Without him I can do nothing. Pride fails to acknowledge God's authority, and his right to do his will in the armies of heaven and the inhabitants of earth.

So insidious is pride that it blinds us to our own sin. It makes us smile disdainfully at our neighbor for his foibles while we, with greater privilege and responsibility, are guilty of deeds far worse than his. It is I, attempting to take from my child's eye a splinter, while I have a log in my own eye. It is you, contemplating the sin of the king of Assyria with scorn and not seeing that you, too, are bypassing God and his will for your life.

And could it be that sometimes we are quite proud of our humility?

Destruction . . . Overwhelming and Righteous

[*Isaiah 10:20–34*]

Pendulum-like, the prophecy focuses again upon the righteous remnant who will be saved. Although this people are to be as the sands of the sea, there will be only a remnant to return from the Babylonian captivity. But they will truly rely upon the Holy One of Israel.

Then, like lightning, verse 22 flashes upon us: 'Destruction has been decreed, overwhelming and righteous!' If the theme of desolation and apparently wanton destruction jars us, as we sometimes find to be the case, we will be brought up short here. The destruction God has decreed may be overwhelming, but it is also *righteous*. Our God does all things well. If he chooses to discipline his own people even as he punishes the godless nations, he does it in righteousness. His holy name must be guarded. Men cannot be allowed to get away with saying, 'How can a just and loving God . . ?' or 'If God is loving, how comes he to allow . . ?' In our sin and ignorance we may feel uncomfortable when we contemplate God's acts of destruction – for example, his spewing out of hot lava from Mount Saint Helens – but we may never look down our noses at him. Nor may we claim a contrast between the God of the Old Testament as full of wrath and the God of the New Testament as so loving. He is one God, unchanging and righteous, whether in his love or his wrath. Both aspects of his nature are seen throughout Scripture.

And there will be a remnant!

God's people were given the promise that soon his anger against them would end and would be directed against their enemies. He would lop off the boughs. He would fell the lofty trees and bring the tall ones low. He would cut down the forest thickets with an axe. Lebanon would fall before him.

Sometimes we shudder as we read the daily newspaper. Viewing television is an awful experience. We feel dwarfed and impotent against the powers of evil that loom on every side. We feel like garden herbs in a forest of redwoods. But God will fell the giant trees. He is sovereign and the workers of evil can go no further than he permits.

One day these forces of wickedness will be completely demolished. Then we will appreciate as never before how very righteous God is when he destroys evil. Had he not destroyed the evil nations around her, how could Judah have survived as his people – or even as a political entity? How could the Old Testament have been written and preserved? How could the line of the Messiah have been guarded? As his church we rejoice that God told the nations that crashed like angry waves upon the shores of Judah, 'Thus far you may come and no farther'.

His destruction is overwhelming and righteous! *Bless his name.*

A Shoot from the Stump of Jesse

[Isaiah 11:1–9]

A number of years ago at a missionary conference near Washington, D.C., a white woman from the Union of South Africa and a black Rhodesian man sang a beautiful duet. You may have heard the chorus they sang:

> *Father, I adore you,*
> *Lay my life before you.*
> *How I love you!*

We who heard this duet experienced the reality of the peaceable kingdom. The Prince of Peace reigns over this kingdom, which extends throughout the world where God's truth has spread. Before our eyes we saw on that occasion the prophecy of Isaiah being fulfilled:

> . . . *the earth will be full of the knowledge of the Lord as the waters cover the sea.*

In chapter 11 Isaiah tells us about the peaceable kingdom and about the one by whom it is to be governed!

In the preceding chapter the prophet had spoken about the felling of great trees, the cutting down of royal power. Even the Davidic line, the line of Jesus, he here implies, will be brought down. But the root and stump of the tree that once stood so proud will remain. Out of that stump will grow a tiny shoot from which will develop a Branch, a sturdy and healthy Branch which will bear fruit. 'In that day,' as we read in chapter 4, 'the Branch of the Lord will be beautiful and glorious, and the fruit of the land will be the pride and glory of the survivors in Israel.'

Isaiah lays aside his botanical figure quickly and dwells upon the nature of the One whom he has called the Branch. God's Spirit dwells in this One – that Spirit whose presence means wisdom, understanding, counsel, power, knowledge and the fear of the Lord. What a detailed and full sketch of Jesus of Nazareth!

He will delight in the fear of the Lord, does Isaiah say? How often Christians inquire the meaning of the fear of the Lord. Here we are told that the Son himself will have that fear and delight in it! What is the fear of the Lord but a recognition of God's holiness and power and the resulting peace and security that his holiness and power make possible? Is not such a recognition a reason for rejoicing? As we are made aware of our sinfulness and weakness we rest more and more in the holiness and power of God. And we delight that such a One will accept us and that he will gently lead us and mould us into the image of his Son. If the Messiah, without a personal weakness or sin, delighted in the fear of the Lord, so much more should we. And as this fear was not an indication of weakness in him, but of strength, so it is in us.

No wonder this Branch will usher in such a kingdom! With omniscience the righteous Judge will make his decisions. The human judge in the court of law is limited in his knowledge and abilities. So are we as day by day we are in a position where we have to make decisions. Those who have served on a jury attest to their uncertainty as they are compelled either to condemn or acquit a human being about whose guilt or innocence they cannot be altogether sure. Our Judge knows all the facts. He knows all the law – it is his law – and he will apply it impartially.

In his kingdom will exist such peace that the wolf and the lamb will live together . . . and 'a little child will lead them'. In God's kingdom men who, throughout history, have been enemies will live together in peace, praising the Father of them both and adoring him.

For the peaceable kingdom is the church. It is the church now, yes, and more intensively and extensively it is the church triumphant. To the extent to which the church abides under the lovely shadow of the Branch today, we rejoice. But we rejoice further that the day will come when the sin that now clings to her will be shaken out like dust from a rug and she will know what real peace and holiness are.

'Amen. Come, Lord Jesus'(Revelation 22:20).

A Banner for the Peoples

[*Isaiah 11:10–16*]

The story of Francis Scott Key, waiting through the long dark night to know how his country fared, and then rejoicing at the dawn's early light to see that his flag was still there, speaks to our hearts about love of country. It speaks to us about flags and banners, and what emotion the sight of them, waving in the breeze, evokes in those over whom they fly!

In the early part of this chapter Isaiah used the figure of the Branch to help people understand something about the coming Messiah. He described the nature of the kingdom to be established by the Branch. In the final verse of our last reading he proclaimed that the kingdom would extend throughout the world, covering the earth 'as the waters cover the sea'.

This last statement, plus the strong emphasis upon the Messiah, is an indication that, although the return from Babylonian exile may be in his mind, Isaiah speaks here of the gospel age. Throughout the chapter his focus is Christ, first figured in the Branch and now in a banner which God will raise for the people.

Among ancient peoples, a banner was not usually a fabric flag but was a carved or molten symbol topping a pole. But the function was the same. The Messiah is represented as a banner to which the nations would rally. At his feet they would find glorious rest.

At that time Israel was pretty well contained in its own land. Isaiah looks into the future and sees world-wide dispersion. He sees the scattered remnant of Israel, the true Israel of God, raising this banner among all the nations. Isaiah projects his message into the distant future, even to our time. We can see men and women from many religious backgrounds, from under the sickle and crescent, as well as the star of David, rallying round the cross. We can hear men and women living under many national flags, blending their tongues and dialects in praise of the Lamb of God who has taken away the sin of the *world*. And the culmination will be when we all gather at the marriage feast of the Lamb in the heavenly Jerusalem.

David speaks about the banner, too. He says that the Lord has given us a banner 'to be unfurled' (Psalm

60:4). This banner, even as a candle, is not to be hidden under a basket. It is to be flown high. That is what a banner is for – to proclaim a cause, to set forth for all to see the principles and purpose of a group of persons, a political entity, a religious organization, a military body. Observe the banners borne by zealots marching down the streets of our great cities setting forth causes they represent. As the banner that God has given is raised on high and flown in the breeze it will be a means of drawing nations to himself.

Moses was instructed to place a brazen serpent high on a pole where all could see. Whoever looked at the serpent would be healed from his snakebite and live. 'I,' said Jesus, 'when I am lifted up from the earth, will draw all men to myself' (John 12:32). Whoever looks to him in faith is healed of his sin and lives eternally. For those who fear God, as David pointed out, the Lord raised a banner and under it they will find salvation from their great enemy.

> *Thank you, Lord, for giving us your banner. Help us to display it in our behavior and in our speech. Help us to acknowledge in all we do the One whose banner we bear.*

The Wells of Salvation

[*Isaiah 12*]

Here are songs of rejoicing: 'The Lord is my strength and my *song* . . . with *joy* you will draw water from the wells of salvation . . . *Sing* to the Lord for he has done glorious things . . . Shout aloud and *sing* for *joy*.' These are our songs, we who were a needy people – dirty, thirsty and sorrowful. God cleanses us from our sin. He satisfies our thirst. With joy we draw water from the wells of salvation.

A person who casually turns on the faucet (tap) in an air-conditioned kitchen has little sense of the impact of these words of Isaiah on the Jews of his day. Isaiah was writing directly to men and women who walked long under the mid-Eastern sun reflected from the hot sands and then revelled at the cool water drawn immediately from a well. As they read his words they could feel the cool refreshment of water moistening their lips and dry throats and splashing on their dusty feet.

Even in Isaiah's day this figure was not adequate to express the joy of the Lord as men experience the salvation of their souls. Words, even the incomparable words of Isaiah, are weak and inadequate. But this side of heaven words have to suffice. And God has given us his Spirit to bring them to life for us.

Later on in his book, especially in chapters 41 and 55, the poet will be speaking more about water. As men come to God with their thirst he will make water flow on barren mountains. He will cause springs to burst forth from parched ground. God will urge men to drink this water. It is free. It is satisfying. It is life-giving!

And further on, in John 4:14, the Lord Jesus himself uses this figure. He is speaking to the woman at the well in Samaria and he says: 'Whoever drinks the water I give him will never thirst. Indeed, the water I give him will become in him a spring of water welling up to eternal life.'

During the Feast of Tabernacles Jesus speaks again

in these terms. At this feast there was a ceremony of water, symbolizing the need of the children of Israel for water as they wandered through the wilderness. The last day of the feast represented the arrival in Canaan where there was water in abundance. On this day the Master-teacher stood up and issued a gracious invitation: 'If a man is thirsty, let him come to me and drink. Whoever believes in me, as the Scripture has said, streams of living water will flow from within him' (John 7:37 and 38). Jesus knew that even in Canaan men would be thirsty for the water which was his to give.

The water in Isaiah and the water of Christ is one – water provided by the Creator himself for the souls of his people. With joy we drink. And with joy we offer this water to those who are thirsty and sinful around us, water from the wells of salvation.

The Lord . . . Mustering an Army

[*Isaiah 13*]

There are some who equate religion and pacifism. To them this chapter, following hard after similar ones, poses a real problem: the Lord mustering an army; the Lord summoning warriors to carry out his wrath; God using Persia and Media to destroy Babylon. It is important that the Christian should attempt to understand these passages. He needs to be able to accept the character of God and to discern the background and intent of his words and actions. With this in mind we shall look at this matter from three perspectives.

First, God is absolute Sovereign. As Creator of all things and all peoples, as the divine potter, he has the right to make some vessels fit for destruction as well as some fit for the master's use. Not one of his creatures can decide what God has the right to do and what he does not have the right to do. And here, in Isaiah, the Lord is mustering an army.

Second, God is holy. In his holiness sin is an offense to him. He cannot abide it. Light and darkness cannot dwell together. So much did he hate sin that he was willing to send his Son to the cross, that his beloved people might be free from sin's penalty and power. So much did he hate sin that he turned his face when his Son was bearing our sin on the cross. People who are living in sin are incurring the righteous wrath of God. And the Lord is mustering an army.

Third, God has a chosen people with whom he identifies himself, the people of his covenant. Babylon, the enemy of Israel, may be used by God for a time to humble this people, to refine them as gold is refined in the furnace of affliction, but eventually God will raise up the Medes and Persians to destroy Babylon because of the harm she has done to his people. Any people who are a threat – physically, morally or spiritually – to God's children may expect wrath.

> *I will bless those who bless you,*
> *and whoever curses you I will curse,*

God said to Abraham (Genesis 12:3). Judas was an instrument of the Lord to bring salvation to God's people as he sold the Son of God for thirty pieces of silver. But Judas experienced God's wrath. And the Lord is mustering an army.

God, we read, will overthrow Babylon:

> *She will never be inhabited*
> *or lived in through all generations.*

The traveller will tell you that this is the case. There is no Babylon today. Not even the tent of one Arab is pitched on the site of the once flourishing city. God accomplished exactly what he declared he would do. His victory over sin is symbolized in the fate of Babylon.

This passage loses its true significance if we do not see that Judah, the Israel of God, signifies the church today. Babylon, the personification of the forces of Satan, is the enemy of the church and of her Bridegroom. Babylon *must* be destroyed. God has the right and power to do this. His holiness requires it. His unity with the Bride demands that this be accomplished against her foe. In his own time, after his own plan, he will do it. And the Lord is mustering an army.

We are the army God is mustering today. Paul in Ephesians 6 has told us what our weapons are and has instructed us to put on the whole armor of God.

O Lord, help us to be thoroughly prepared for the conflict that is iife. Thank you for the assurance of victory.

How You Have Fallen from Heaven

[Isaiah 14:1–23]

Babylon is finally to be destroyed for the sake of Judah. The house of Israel is to be settled in her own land. She is to be comforted by her Covenant God. She has the promise from him that she will reach out into the nations.

In this chapter there is, according to Joseph Addison Alexander, what has been considered 'one of the finest specimens of Hebrew and indeed of ancient composition.' The destruction of Babylon is focused in the death of her king. Isaiah foretells the relief that the earth will experience at his death and at the laying low of Babylonian power. Whether Belshazzar is referred to here or whether, as E. J. Young prefers, the reference is not to one specific person but to the Babylonian dynasty, the force is the same. The rest and peace of all the lands is expressed in the words of the pines and cedars to the fallen king:

> *Now that you have been laid low,*
> *no woodsman comes to cut us down.*

There is relief on the earth. And what about in the grave? In verses 9, 10 and 11 Isaiah takes us to Sheol, the abode of the dead. In his imagination he powerfully pictures those who have been rulers in the earth rising from their thrones at the entrance of the king of

Babylon and addressing him. They remind him that, like themselves, even he had become weak.

The king is addressed thus:

> *All your pomp has been brought down to the grave,*
> *along with the noise of your harps;*
> *Maggots are spread out beneath you*
> *and worms cover you.*

From worms was extracted a scarlet dye which was used for bed covers. The poet was undoubtedly drawing a parallel and contrast indelicate to our ears, perhaps, between the covers on the bed of the living monarch and the covers on the one in the grave.

Isaiah goes on to speak to the king. You have sought to raise your throne above the stars and to be like God. Now you have fallen from heaven to earth. You who would not let your captives go home are dead. You lie still unburied. What a shame to a monarch! This shame was the lot of Belshazzar, who was not given a burial.

Our thoughts may turn to the words of Jesus in Luke 10:18, 'I saw Satan fall like lightning from heaven,' and to the words of John in Revelation 12, describing the great dragon Satan who deceived the whole world and then was cast down from heaven to earth.

Not only does the king of Babylon call to mind what we read concerning Satan, but Babylon herself calls to mind passages which refer to the kingdom of Satan. At the conclusion of Peter's first Epistle, the name *Babylon* is used to refer to this kingdom. One-time center of civilization, Babylon becomes a symbol for ungodly world power. Peter uses this designation for Rome, it is thought, in order to protect the saints there from the persecution Christians were experiencing from the enemies of the gospel.

John uses the word *Babylon* for the woman gorgeously dressed but having in her hand the cup of abominable things. On her forehead, he says, is written, 'Mystery, Babylon the Great, the Mother of Prostitutes and of the Abominations of the earth' (Revelation 17:5). Surely the world powers that are set against God are personified in this woman! She was drunk with the blood of Christians.

Even as Babylon and her king fell, so all the ungodly world system and the very spirit of ungodliness will fall. As we read in Daniel 5:26, God wrote upon the wall for Belshazzar to read:

> . . . *God has numbered the days of your reign*
> *and brought it to an end.*
> . . . *You have been weighed on the scales and*
> *found wanting.*
> . . . *Your kingdom is divided.*

And he wrote it for Satan to read.

As I Have Planned, So It Will Be

[Isaiah 14:24–32]

We have plans and are forced to abandon them. A teacher carefully prepares her lesson plan knowing full well that she may have to depart from it. As Robert Burns of Scotland wrote:

> *The best laid schemes o' mice an' men*
> *Gang aft a-gley.*

But the plans of God are not so. Verses 24 to 27 here are a magnificent declaration of God's sovereignty. As he planned it, so it will be. As he purposed, so it will stand. His purposes are settled. They are far more secure than even the proverbial laws of the Medes and the Persians!

From a prophecy of God's cutting off of Babylon, Isaiah here returns to the enemy to be cut off in the nearer future. He states God's plan to cut off the Assyrians in his own land, to trample them down on God's own mountain. When we get to Isaiah 37 we shall read the story as it occurred. Sennacherib was put to confusion just outside the city of Jerusalem and he and his armies fled in terror. Sennacherib and the hosts of the Assyrians had come down

> *like the wolf on the fold,*
> *And his cohorts were gleaming in purple and gold.*

But it was not God's plan for him to conquer Judah. As Lord Byron goes on to express it,

> *. . . the widows of Ashur are loud in their wail,*
> *And the idols are broke in the temple of Baal;*
> *And the might of the Gentile, unsmote by the sword,*
> *Hath melted like snow in the glance of the Lord!*

God's plan, however, encompasses far more than the destruction of the Assyrian or yet the Babylonian. His design is determined for the whole world of ungodly nations. An all-knowing, all-powerful God must by his very character have an all-embracing plan. This cannot be controverted by any man. For the Lord Almighty has purposed, we read, and who can thwart him? His hand is stretched out, and who can turn it back?

The plan of an all-wise, loving God cannot be purely negative, bent upon putting down the wicked. What is its driving, over-riding purpose? The positive purpose of God's plan is the establishment of his people for his own glory. In verse 28 we are turned to an oracle which is directed against the Philistines, who had taken several cities in southern Judah in the reign of Ahaz. The oracle concludes with this resounding note:

> *The Lord has established Zion,*
> *And in her his afflicted people will find refuge.*

The Lord has established Zion, his church, the people for whom his Son died. Jesus has promised that the gates of Assyria, Philistia, yes, the gates of hell, shall not prevail against her. His church is indestructible; her establishment is the very heart of God's plan. Not one of those entrusted to him will be lost!

> *Surely, as I have planned, so it will be (v.24).*

My Heart Cries Out over Moab

[Isaiah 15]

In unmitigated gloom and terror the fate of Moab is pictured. There is no gleam of hope filtering through the darkness of this elegy. With majestic cadence (which the NIV retains), line after line piles up to produce the impact of total loss.

God was bent upon preserving his people. Part of that preservation necessarily lay in protecting them against Moab. We are better able to comprehend his destruction of this people when we become aware of her history.

The story begins in a cave in the mountains, but we go further back than that. Lot, the once-wealthy nephew of Abraham, chose to live in Sodom – to raise his two daughters in the wicked city whose name still is used to describe sexual degenerates. Through God's messengers Lot was warned that God was going to destroy the city. Lot attempted to convince the men to whom his daughters were engaged to flee the city with him, but they mocked him. So Lot, his wife and the girls alone escaped the doom of Sodom. And Lot's wife, defying God by looking back, was transformed into a pillar of salt.

God's angels told Lot to flee to the mountains. He was afraid to do this and prayed instead to be permitted to go to a certain town called Zoar. 'It is a little city,' he argued and God granted his request. Then, although God promised that he would not overthrow Zoar, Lot became afraid and fled to the mountains.

So here we are in the mountains where he lived with his two daughters. Miserable Lot! God had been gracious to him, but he was forgetful and weak. What kind of father had he been to his daughters in Sodom? The evidence is against him. And now comes the saddest incident in his life. The two girls, having no opportunity for marriage here in the wilds, plotted together to get their father drunk, to have sexual intercourse with him and to bear him children. Then, as Genesis 19:37 records, 'The older daughter had a son, and she named him Moab; he is the father of the

Moabites of today.' From a man born of incest there grew up a people, close to Abraham though they were, who were far from Abraham and his God. This is the people that God, in pursuit of his plan to preserve Israel, had to destroy.

However, later God in his grace blessed Moab with a singular honor. By his grace Ruth, a Moabite girl, was chosen to be an ancestress of king David. Matthew records her name in the royal line of the Messiah.

Even here in this chapter and in the one following we see that the heart of God is not untouched by the fate Moab is to endure. The words, 'My heart cries out over Moab,' may be the fancied words of a grieving Moabite or they may be the words of Isaiah himself. But we see them as indeed the words of the God who takes no pleasure in the death of the wicked.

Our God is not the merciless, unfeeling despot some would paint him. He is not one who is untouched by the infirmities of men. His personality is not fragmented: in and through all the destruction which his justice and holiness required him to inflict upon sinful men there is tenderness.

Remember how God chided Jonah for his unfeeling attitude toward Nineveh? God's heart cried out over Moab the way it did over Nineveh. And the heart of his Son cried out over the city of Jerusalem.

What about our hearts? Do they cry out over Middletown . . . and New York . . . and Moscow . . . and London?

In Love a Throne Will Be Established

[Isaiah 16]

Moab's fate is assured. In three years, measured as exactly as the years of a servant bound by contract are measured, she will be destroyed (v. 14).

It is too late for repentance. God's plan will not be changed. Nevertheless Moab is told to send the tribute to Zion that is due. Moab, you see, had been subdued by the kingdom of David and had been tributary to Israel. In 2 Kings 3:4 we read that the king of Moab had sent a hundred thousand lambs and the wool of as many rams to the king of Israel. This she is being told still to do, but such an outward sign of submission will not be counted pleasing to God, the ruler of the land, without the submission of a contrite spirit. Moab's fate is sealed.

Moab pleads with Judah, asking that when her people come to her as fugitives Judah will hide them, protecting them as a comforting shadow shields men from the scorching mid-day sun. She asks for acceptance from God's people. Moab, the proud one who has no claim to Judah's protection, asks Judah to be a haven to her fleeting remnant who will be pushed from the nest like fluttering birds. Sela, the *rock*, was that seemingly impregnable natural fortress to the south of the Dead Sea which we know as Petra. Protect us as we flee from the fortress we thought always would be safe, Moab is saying.

As Moab would seek mercy from Judah she would be acknowledging the nature of the 'ruler of the land' who dwells in Zion. Here in Judah, the inference is, a throne will indeed be established *in love*. A king will reign from David's line, who will judge justly and speed the cause of righteousness.

'In love a throne will be established!' What an incongruous phrase is this in the context of international affairs! We might expect the prophet to say that *in power* or *in might* a throne will be established. But no, it is in love.

Isaiah's immediate reference may have been to Hezekiah, who surely strove to rule justly and to speed the cause of righteousness. But see here ultimate reference to the King from the house of David who came riding upon an ass in the company of men and women and boys and girls whom he loved – feeding them, healing them, teaching them and even raising some of them from the dead. Know that it was love that drove this King to leave his heavenly glory and be born a man. It was love that enabled him to experience death – even separation from his Father – that we might not have to die eternally.

The gates of the city of God are open today to fugitives who will come in humility to the King who rules in love. But the proud, who would come under their own terms, will meet the fate of Moab. Not accepting the terms of God Almighty, they plead in vain to their own gods, but will just wear themselves out. When they go to their shrines to pray it will be to no avail.

Even as we are angered by peoples who scorn the proffers of love of our God, do we not also lament for Moab like a harp? The King who occupies the throne in

love teaches us to maintain this tension. And he will
enable us to do so.

Tumbleweed[1]

[Isaiah 17]

Naaman had asked the prophet Elisha, 'Are not
Abana and Pharpar, rivers of Damascus, better than all
the waters of Israel?' (2 Kings 5:12). Damascus will be
destroyed. She will be a heap of ruins.

But it will not end there. Step by step God brings
judgment closer home to his people: Damascus, Aram,
Ephraim. Now he speaks to Israel, whom he here calls
Jacob. He contrasts the strength and vigor of the man
Jacob with the wasting away of his descendants. He
likens the coming judgments upon Israel, as she is
carried away by the Assyrians, to the shaking of an olive
tree to harvest its fruit for oil. He pictures the tree
stripped except for a half dozen olives. These gleanings
that remain speak of those few of Jacob who survive in
Palestine when all the rest are taken captive.

'Oh', used twice in verse 12, E. J. Young tells us, is the
heart-cry of Isaiah – 'Alas . . . alas' – as he contemplates
the looting and plundering of Jacob. He says that a
person who reads this verse aloud in Hebrew several
times will be stirred by the language used to describe the
advance of an overpowering, onrushing sea. This is the
Assyrian army bearing down upon Jerusalem.

[1]The American name for any kind of plant whose upper part becomes
detached from the roots and is blown about by the wind.

But at the gates of the city the enemy halts. Isaiah's figure changes. No longer is the Assyrian army a raging sea. Now it is like chaff – tumbleweed! By morning the wind has blown it away. The Assyrians, who come in might and power, meet with the invisible power of Israel's God. And, as Isaiah says, 'Before the morning, they are gone!'

David uses the figure of tumbleweed, too, in Psalm 83:13. In speaking of God's enemies, he prays,

> *Make them like tumbleweed, O my God,*
> *like chaff before the wind . . .*
> *Cover their faces with shame*
> *so that men will seek your name, O Lord.*

Have you ever seen tumbleweed? To one reared in an Eastern city in the United States the first sight of tumbleweed was of great interest. I had never seen as much as a picture of this phenomenon or read a description of it. Only the fragment of Bob Nolan's haunting song lodged in my memory from my youth in the thirties: 'Drifting along with the tumbling tumbleweeds.'

Then, as an adult driving through the fields of Iowa for the first time, I saw the dry, leafless skeleton of a plant, disengaged from the roots, and rolling like a ball over the bare field in the breeze. I immediately burst out, 'That has to be tumbleweed!' And the poet's figure takes on special significance as we picture an army, proceeding with all its might, suddenly become impotent, 'driven before the wind like chaff on the hills.'

Isaiah spoke of the day when men would look to their Maker and turn their eyes to the Holy One of Israel. If our eyes rest upon our Maker where they belong, we will not fear what men, though they appear to be powerful as the Assyrians, might do to us.

[68]

Christians, do not underestimate your God. When the enemy comes catapulting upon you, remember that the mere breath of your God can turn him into tumbleweed and he will be gone.

Land of Whirring Wings

[Isaiah 18]

Cush is ancient Ethiopia. It was a land of whirring wings – of the dreaded zetse flies, perhaps, but wings of hordes of armies as well! For her men were aggressive, feared far and wide. These men were tall and smooth of skin. (Herodotus claimed that every third day the priests of Egypt, a neighboring country, shaved their whole body.) Men with a language strange to the Jews.

Cush was a land of commerce with the White Nile and Blue Nile, the Atbara and Tacazze Rivers. Her boats of papyrus, resistant to rapids, braved the rough waters at the sources of these rivers and sailed into the quiet Nile to the north and on into the Mediterranean.

Historic details are lacking and Isaiah's figurative language leaves us wondering about identities. Probably Isaiah is saying that in these boats Cush is sending envoys to distant places, perhaps Assyria. Although she is powerful, Cush fears a nation more powerful still, Assyria. And she is making efforts to ward off a southern march of Assyria to her land.

For Cush herself God has a message: it will not be through your efforts, but through God himself, that Cush will be spared. It will be through him, invisible as

THE WELLS OF SALVATION

heat and benign as a cloud, that the Assyrians will be halted in their invasions. Indeed, Assyria's plans will be allowed to develop, like grapes ripening on a branch, with God's warmth and dew assisting in their matura-tion. And then, when it is almost time for the harvest, God will

> . . . *cut off the shoots with pruning knives*
> *and cut down and take away the spreading branches.*

As God spares Judah he will also spare Cush. The Assyrians, like tumbleweed, will be blown away.

2 Chronicles 32:22 and 23 may throw light on verse 7. We read that the Lord saved Jerusalem from Assyria and from all others. 'Many brought offerings to Jerusalem for the Lord and valuable gifts for Hezekiah king of Judah. From then on he was highly regarded by all the nations.' Cush, spared by Judah's God, would bring her gifts with the rest.

As we see the unfolding of history we can glory in God's subsequent dealings with Ethiopia. We can see his banner raised. Think of the day God sent his messenger Philip to meet an important official in charge of the treasury of Queen Candace. This man had been in Jerusalem worshiping. In his capacity as treasurer was he also bringing gifts from Cush? His worship was a gift surpassing any others. On his way home he was sitting in his chariot reading this very book of Isaiah. He was reading in chapter fifty-three, verse 7, of one who 'was led like a lamb to the slaughter, and as a sheep before her shearers is silent, so he did not open his mouth.' Philip began at that verse, as we read in Acts 8:26–39, and told the Ethiopian eunuch about the Lord Jesus. The man was baptized and went home with his precious scroll of Isaiah and with water from the wells of salvation. Did he show Candace the very section we are reading? Did she listen to his testimony? Did she, too, send gifts to the Place of the Name of the Almighty?

Today Ethiopia proper does not welcome God's messengers from outside, but inside her borders there are the faithful ones who in the face of persecution are worshiping the true God. Even in our country small groups of Ethiopians gather to worship. And Abyssinia, a part of ancient Ethiopia, is a Christian nation, nominally at least.

One day even more Ethiopians, along with men from all over the globe, will hear the trumpet and come into the church where God dwells with his people. They will come presenting themselves a living sacrifice.

Egypt My People, Assyria My Handiwork

[*Isaiah 19*]

When Isaiah wrote, the monuments of Egypt were old. The children of Israel – perhaps 750 years before – had slaved to build some of them. Many dated back before their time. The Temple of Karnak, the Sphinxes, the Pyramids were familiar by report at least in Isaiah's time just as they are today.

The oracle tells us that the Lord will come to Egypt and that these idols (for such they truly were) will tremble before him. The presence of God will so thoroughly agitate the land that monuments weighing several tons and constructed to endure three thousand years may be said to tremble! What a figure of the powerlessness and ultimate destruction of idolatry in the face of God's truth! The hearts of the Egyptians will melt within them. Or, as E. J. Young translates these words, even *the heart of Egypt* herself will melt within her.

Judah in time of threats from without was wont to rely on Egypt. Isaiah wants her to see the folly of this and to understand that Egypt, too, is vulnerable. In this chapter, by presenting very specific problems that will be Egypt's, the prophet warns Judah of the frailty of her ally. He speaks of civil discord and the overthrow of leadership. The wisdom she boasted of at the time of Moses will be gone. And the Nile, which was the source of all her life, will dry up. What a symbol this is of her collapse! The Romans used to say *Aut Nilus, aut nihil* – 'Either the Nile or nothing.' If the Nile were gone, all Egypt would fall.

Commentators believe we should not search history for specific events that were fulfilments of these prophecies of gloom. They believe this is a composite picture of the downfall of Egypt.

Similarly they consider the next section to be a composite picture of what has happened through history, pointing to the penetration of the gospel in Egypt. Isaiah wanted now to encourage his readers in their Lord and his power over the nations.

How strange these words of Isaiah must have sounded to those who were used to being referred to as God's own special people, distinct from the heathen nations of the world! The prophet was giving them a glimpse of the gospel age. They were seeing, though they were understanding so little, the bringing of good news to the ends of the earth, even to Egypt and Assyria, symbols of the mighty nations of the world –

Gentile nations. They were seeing, in shadow, Athanasius and the thriving church in Alexandria in the early Christian era. They were seeing the Coptic Church through the years, distorting the truth, yes, but possessing it and today awaking in some small degree to the wonder of the treasures they have been hiding under a bushel for so long. They were seeing the Egypt of today, spawning ground for the church of Christ as men and women are coming to him and as Bibles and fine Christian literature are being distributed. They were seeing God's healing, as Alexandria draws to herself from all over Africa young men who are learning the truth at the feet of his servants.

What more they were seeing we cannot say, because we, like them, have yet to witness these amazing words of Isaiah come to full reality in God's good time. But this we know: we may expect to see God's grace showered abroad, and Egypt and Assyria, these ancient enemies, making peace with God and with his people and so finding peace with each other. Even as this book is being written, the American Back to God Hour (with Bassam Madany, an Arab, and Victor Atallah, an Egyptian), is bearing witness to the truth to thousands of persons in the Near East. What an honor God grants us to participate in this witness that God is using to bring his truth to Egypt today!

Verse 25 has been called by J. A. Alexander 'one of the clearest and most striking predictions of the calling of the Gentiles that the Word of God contains.' 'Egypt, my people,' God says. 'Assyria, my handiwork!' You, yes, but also Iran and Libya and Indo-China, right along with Israel, my inheritance!

How Then Can We Escape?

[Isaiah 20]

Faith, it has been said, is an invisible means of support. And for the children of men, to trust in anything invisible is most difficult. No matter how weak a bush struggling for life along the rugged mountain path may be, we grasp it for support as our feet slip from under us. God would teach us to trust in *him*. His Branch, although invisible to the naked eye, is the only one that will support us.

The supreme Assyrian commander, sent from King Sargon, had come to Ashdod in Philistia. He was on his way to Egypt and Ethiopia. His capture of Ashdod was a portent of his overcoming these two nations in whom Israel had been trusting.

God spoke to Isaiah. He gave him a humiliating role to play. Isaiah, of royal blood and refined taste, was to take off his usual outer garments (probably he was wearing sackcloth as a sign of grief over the state of his beloved country) and his sandals. For three years he was to go around stripped and barefoot, as an object lesson for his people. Thus, he was to tell them, will Egyptians and Ethiopians, with buttocks bared to their shame, be led away by the Assyrians.

And those who trust in them will be put to shame, too. Israel, who had been putting her trust in men and not in God, would see the weak bush along the mountain path give way as she was grasping it for support. Israel would say, 'See what happened to those we relied upon! See what happened to those we fled to for help and deliverance against the king of Assyria! How then can we escape?'

How long would it take Israel to learn that in her weakness her only escape was her God?

Isaiah, wandering around naked and barefoot, is a sign for God's church today. He is a picture of world leaders who, we may think, are our allies. He is a picture of political parties which we think are sharing our priorities. He is a picture of everything save God himself that we may be relying upon against our common enemy, Satan. God may be using Isaiah today to warn his people against dealing with their weakness foolishly.

Paul had a weakness, a thorn in the flesh. He went to God about it, asking him to remove it. God's words to him are to us, too: 'My grace is sufficient for you, for my power is made perfect in weakness' (2 Corinthians 12:9). When we recognize and acknowledge our finiteness and come to the Infinite One, then we are strong.

He offers us salvation through his Son. 'How shall we escape,' the writer of Hebrews asks, 'if we ignore such a great salvation?' (2:3).

As Peter said to Jesus, 'Lord, to whom shall we go? You have the words of eternal life' (John 6:68).

I Tell You What I Have Heard from the Lord

[Isaiah 21]

Isaiah's task in life was a gruelling one. Not only was he subjected to the isolating and humiliating experience of walking around stripped and barefoot for three years, but all his career he received from God visions of desolation. Must he not have become deeply depressed at times as he had to relay to the people the substance of these visions?

So it is here with the prophecies concerning the fate of Babylon and Edom and Arabia. It was a dire vision shown him of Babylon – to be laid low by the Medo-Persian army. So dire was the vision that his body was racked with pain. Pangs seized him 'like those of a woman in labor.' He was staggered by what he heard and bewildered by what he saw. He had nightmares that troubled his sleep. This calamity was to be visited upon the enemy of God's people, yes, but its impact would cause any sensitive fellow human being to tremble.

Actually Isaiah did not live to see God perform this destruction of Babylon. It came to pass under Cyrus of Persia in 539 B.C. But to Isaiah it was real. 'Babylon has fallen, has fallen!' he heard the man in the chariot say. And the very thought of it gave him much pain.

Did Isaiah shrink from telling these visions and oracles? No! What he heard from the Lord Almighty he told. The God of Israel had spoken to him. This was all that was necessary to compel him to speak. One day he had said to God, 'Here am I, send me!' Never did he retract these words.

The boy Samuel had been given difficult words from God to speak to the aged Eli. He struggled within himself. He was afraid to tell Eli the vision. But because the message had come from God he delivered it.

The Christian, were he to dwell continually upon sin and its consequences, would be, like Isaiah, in continual pain. His heart would falter, and fear would make him tremble. But the Lord has given us, as he gave Isaiah, strong words to declare. We have assurance that indeed in Scripture the Almighty Lord is speaking. We have no choice but to relay to men what the Holy Spirit has revealed.

Our message, though it has good news for those who believe, has, like Isaiah's, a stern warning that makes it unpopular. Do we have the courage to say, 'I tell you what I have heard from the Lord Almighty'? Do we pray for our pastor that he may tell us freely and fearlessly what God reveals in his Word?

In a sense morning is here with the Sun of Righteousness dispelling the night of sin in this world. And our God *is* sovereign. But in another sense we do live in the night: all of existence here on earth is night in contrast to the eternal day when God the Light will have driven away all darkness for ever.

And there is a place of eternal night apart from God.

We are standing on the watchtower. We see the enemy of men's souls rallying his forces. Sinners need to be warned. God's people need to be alerted. Those of us who have been entrusted with God's words need to speak what we have heard!

The Valley of Vision

[Isaiah 22:1–14]

The oracles of Isaiah had been dealing with Assyria and Babylonia, the Philistines, Moab, Egypt and Ethiopia, and the destruction that would befall them. In this chapter the prophecy concerns the Valley of Vision.

The Valley of Vision was Jerusalem. Some commentators believe that this name was given to Jerusalem because here a number of times God had appeared in vision to Isaiah and other prophets before him. This is true, of course. But see also in this appellation a deeper meaning. God had given Jerusalem sight. Through the years he had led his people, by Abraham, by Isaac and by Jacob. He was with them in Egypt from Joseph to Moses. He had brought them out of bondage, providing laws and worship for them. He had brought them into Canaan and established them in their own land. He had given them this city, Jerusalem. And through all this experience there had been a vision that had given them hope.

Not only was the vision that of a promised land in Canaan. It was of a worldwide kingdom under Immanuel, the promised King of David's line. And the vision projected them to the very end of time, to the New Jerusalem! They were – we are – a people who dwell in the Valley of Vision.

Often God's people were not faithful to the God who

had given them this vision. So he speaks here of preparing

> . . . *a day*
> *of tumult and trampling and terror*
> *in the Valley of Vision.*

He says that their fear will be so great that they will tear down their houses to strengthen the walls of their city so that they may be protected against their enemies. But they will not regard the One who planned it all. They will not mourn the sin that brought about God's judgment.

God was warning them of captivity. Did he also have in mind the destruction of their temple in 70 A.D.? Was he also warning them of the dispersion of the Jews who refused the King he promised?

We who now dwell in the Valley of Vision have all the revelation they had and much more. We know from our own experience and from history God's work in bringing the gospel to all people. Your inclusion and ours within this Valley was probably brought about through missionaries to the Continent of Europe and the British Isles many centuries ago. And the complete realization of the vision is nearer to us than it was to them.

At Pentecost Peter reminded the people of the words of the prophet Joel:

> *In the last days, God says,*
> *I will pour out my Spirit on all people.*
> *Your sons and your daughters will prophesy,*
> *your young men will see visions,*
> *your old men will dream dreams (Acts 2:17).*

God's Spirit has been poured out. Everyone who comes to Christ is saved. And how great are the conquests we have seen of God's grace! We are a people of vision indeed. Not the kind of vision Isaiah had when the hot coal was placed on his lips. Not the kind of vision Peter had when the sheet was let down before him from heaven. But a vision from the Written Word of God's plan for his people through time and eternity, made vivid to us by the Spirit. A vision that propels us forward to do the will and work of our God.

Thank you, our Lord, for the vision you have given us. Help us not to be as those who lived in Jerusalem of old who, though they lived in the Valley of Vision, failed to look to the One who was establishing the city and building the church. Give us faith in you who planned it long ago. Pour out your Spirit upon us in all fulness!

The Peg Driven into the Firm Place

[*Isaiah 22:15–25*]

The steward Shebna, who was in charge of the palace, was a disgrace to his office. God purposes to depose him. He was expecting to die in high honor and had prepared for himself a tomb in the royal burial place on the mountain. But God told Isaiah to warn him that the Lord would roll him up tightly as a ball and throw him into a wide country. The day did come when he was removed from his post and became merely a private secretary, a position of much less significance in the realm.

In Shebna's place would be set Eliakim, the son of Hilkiah. Shebna's robe and authority would belong to Eliakim. Eliakim would be a father to the people of Jerusalem and Judah. His position would be secure. And all the glory of his father Hilkiah would be granted to him.

At first blush we sense a Messianic ring in this prophecy concerning Shebna and Eliakim. We could see Shebna as Satan, claiming great power for himself but being deposed by God. We could see Eliakim as Christ, given authority and honor in the church: Christ, on whose shoulder the key of the house of David is placed ('What he opens no one can shut. What he shuts no one can open'); Christ, driven by God like a peg into a firm place; Christ, being granted the throne; Christ, upon whom all honor hangs.

But there is a change in the prophecy. The day will come when this peg which has been driven into the firm place will give way and all the honor hanging on it will be cut down. The Messianic parallel falls down and we are brought back to Eliakim. One day Eliakim, who was a mere man, would no longer be steward in the king's palace. (E. J. Young believes the position itself was abolished.) No flesh, even the highly respected Eliakim, may glory in God's sight for ever as the Messiah will. No earthly powers, even pegs which we had thought were driven into firm places, will endure before the coming of the Lord. All powers will fall, the honor hanging from them being cut down.

What folly it is to elevate ourselves, cutting graves for ourselves among the mighty! What folly to take the chief seat at the banquet table!

[81]

God will honor whom he chooses. Ours is the duty to obey him and serve him in integrity and humility and to let any honoring be his initiative.

And what a comfort and security we may find who know Christ and trust in him for eternal salvation! We are truly like a peg driven in a firm place. We are secure eternally.

Thank you, our God, for this security we have in you. Thank you that the vicissitudes of life cannot shake us loose. No one can snatch us out of your hand.

Wail, O Ships of Tarshish

[*Isaiah 23*]

Much of the early history of the 'old, old city' of Tyre lies hidden from the eyes of modern man. She was probably the first city on the coast of the Mediterranean, some twenty-two miles south of Sidon. Later she moved off shore on to two islands in the sea.

At this advantageous location a center of trade was built up, Tyre establishing trade routes to the far places of the world. Of course there was commerce with her neighbors, Sidon and Cyprus. Isaiah speaks also of the ships of Tarshish which frequented her ports. The term *ships of Tarshish* originally referred to any ship from Tarshish or that sailed there. It is uncertain whether Tarshish was off the coast of Africa or whether it was near Gibraltar. However that may be, later the term *ships of Tarshish* came to be used for any large, first-class vessels built for long-distance travel. This type of ship was a common sight to the people of Tyre. Tradition has it that sailors from Tyre plied their trade as far as the British Isles. Some say that her ships rounded the southern tip of Africa. Tyre became the marketplace of the world. Her traders are called princes because of their wealth.

And Tyre was proud of all this. Ezekiel, who gives even more place to Tyre than Isaiah does, represents her as boasting, 'I am perfect in beauty' (Ezekiel 27:3). And in Ezekiel 28:2 the prophet quotes the Lord as saying to her:

> *In the pride of your heart*
> *you say, I am a god;*
> *I sit on the throne of a god*
> *in the heart of the seas.*

For this pride God planned to bring Tyre low and humble her. It is this humbling, probably at the hands of Nebuchadnezzar in the sixth century B.C., that is referred to here. It is this humbling of Tyre that brought anguish to Egypt when she heard it, knowing that if the Assyrians had reached Tyre in their expansion they would soon reach her.

But, while Tyre will again trade with the nations and her pockets will be full once more, this time her profits will go to those who live to fear the Lord and will be set aside for him. Commentators have difficulty in identifying this reference. Some say it speaks of renewed trade with Israel which will profit God's people. Others, such as Calvin, point to the early existence of a colony of Christians in Tyre. The ship on which Paul was sailing to Palestine unloaded cargo at Tyre and he had seven days of precious fellowship with the disciples there. They tried to dissuade him from continuing on his trip and when he was ready to embark they followed him to the seaside – men, women and children participating in a farewell prayer meeting for him. In the fourth century a basilica was erected on Tyre, where it flourished for some three hundred years until it was captured by the Moslems.

God humbled Tyre. At present there is but a small village where she had stood so proudly. Tyre is a place where fishermen dry their nets. The ships of Tarshish have no business there; nor do they wail for her. Again she is a prostitute forgotten. As these lines are being written, Israeli troops have forced their way through Tyre. From time to time she is in the news – but just in a passing reference.

So it must be with all proud nations whose God is not the Lord. Let us pray for our own nation that she may humble herself before God has to humble her.

The Earth – Defiled by Its People

[Isaiah 24]

Isaiah has been prophesying specifically concerning doom for Babylon, Assyria, Egypt and Tyre – even for Judah herself. In this chapter he embraces all of these nations, plus untold nations of which he could not even dream. This is a vision of judgment for the whole earth.

E. J. Young is very convincing in the way in which he brings out the implications here of universality. The whole world of men has transgressed divine law, beginning with the first man and woman. 'There is no one righteous,' wrote Paul; 'Jews and Gentiles alike are all under sin' (Romans 3:9, 10).

Just as the transgression is universal, so is the curse. God's judgment pronounced in Eden was upon all mankind. Isaiah sees in this vision how 'the curse will devour the entire earth' (Young).

How does the clause, 'Its people must bear their guilt,' strike you? Might this not indicate that men are contributing toward their own destruction by blatantly disregarding God's laws? Men all around us are destroying themselves by the neglect and even abuse of their bodies, minds and souls. Men and women are destroying their own seed, some before and some after birth. Might not God be using them as weapons against themselves?

Isaiah sees destruction upon the physical earth as well as upon her inhabitants. Might not men be contributing toward the demise of their planet by their own greed and the repudiation of their stewardship of creation? Here in Maine fish are dying in our lakes. Some believe they are victims of acid rain infected by manufacturing wastes poured into the skies from smoke stacks in states west of us. And wetlands are being filled in for commercial use, depriving sea life of the plants and animals upon which it depends for food. We may be seeing the curse of Eden slowly consuming the earth, a curse for which we ourselves are responsible. If atomic weapons should get out of hand, this process would be ever so much more rapid.

Although many people are destroyed upon the earth, by God's grace some are spared. In verse 13 the familiar simile of the gleanings is used. The remnant are those who will survive the final judgment. And it is this remnant, found from one end of the earth to the other, who raise their voices and give glory to God.

But those on the earth who reject God will not be able to escape his judgment.

What specific form God's judgment will take is not spelled out. Whatever means he uses, however, will be catastrophic and complete:

> *The earth is broken up,*
> *the earth is split asunder,*
> *the earth is thoroughly shaken.*

We have some intimations of the destruction that can be wreaked by natural forces as we see on television how the elements have torn our coastlines, how waters have poured down mountainsides and rendered men homeless. In a field in Iowa we saw lava dust carried there by the wind from the spewings of Mount Saint Helens some 1,400 miles away. 'The earth sways like a hut in the wind . . . It falls – never to rise again.'

Verses 21 and 22 record the consummation of the Lord's dealings with the powers and authorities, his making a public spectacle of them, his completion of the triumphing which he began at the cross. And this judgment includes those among men and angels alike who have been at war against the Lamb. These are bound as prisoners are bound, 'shut up in a prison' from which there is no escape.

When judgment is complete and the powers of sin have been dealt with, then the reign of 'the Lord Almighty' will be shown as all-embracing. And the church with its elders will rejoice in him who reigns over them gloriously. Before the new heavens and the new earth the moon and the sun will be ashamed, for the glory of the coming day will surpass all former glory (compare Isaiah 60:19–20).

In that day the people of God will have nothing but praise for him, because they will know that it was their own sin that brought judgment and that the earth was defiled because of her people. They will worship him for saving them from this judgment through his Son.

The Shroud That Enfolds All Peoples

[*Isaiah 25*]

We are interested to see the attention that is being given today to death and dying. There are courses on the subject and books galore. But regardless of how death is treated in the seminar or the press, and especially in the hospital room, its sting is still there. If its imminence is toned down, this is falsehood. Death is real. It is ugly. And it is unnatural, an event to be dreaded by creatures made for life. Death is a shroud that is wrapped around all people, Isaiah says. Or possibly, the reference is to the veil which is worn by the bereaved. It hangs over all mankind as a grim reminder of mortality.

But God has dealt with death. Isaiah tells us about it here.

God chose for himself a people which he called by his name. He carefully guarded and guided and instructed Israel. Through his appointments for worship and through their prophets he prepared them for One who

would be born who would be God with them –
Immanuel. In him would be all blessings, even the
swallowing up of death.

But when Scripture tells us of the special people it
also tells us that God will include men among them
from *all* nations. His house was to be called a house of
prayer for all peoples and in a significant way when the
Son of God came this fact was realized. We read in
verse 6 that the Lord will prepare a sumptuous feast
for all peoples. With this figure he tells us that his
boundless grace will be displayed for the nourishment
and delight of the souls of men far beyond the walls of
Jerusalem.

Not only does the gracious Father feed all people
with a banquet of the best of meats and the finest of
wines, but he also takes away from them the thing they
most dread, namely, death. He 'swallows up death for
ever'. 'He wipes away the tears from all faces'. He
'removes the disgrace of his people from all the earth'.

It is this very feast that is the means of the destruction of death. It is in the giving of the life of his Son
that life is secured for his people. The Lord Jesus
himself is the feast. When he passed the bread to the
twelve he told them, 'Take and eat; this is my body.'
When he passed the cup to them he said, 'Drink from
it, all of you' (Matthew 26:26, 27).

The death of Jesus accomplished the destruction of
death for his people. Isaiah speaks of this prophetic-
ally. Paul, in 1 Corinthians 15:54, expresses the
accomplishment this way: 'Death has been swallowed
up in victory.' And in the next verse he quotes Hosea:

> *Where, O death, is your victory?*
> *Where, O death, is your sting?*

He goes on to thank God who gives us the victory over death through Christ. And John, in Revelation 21:5, reminds us again about the wiping away of tears as he announces the day when death will be completely destroyed.

Let us not restrict Isaiah's meaning of the word 'death' as mentioned here to the pain and sorrow and separation that make it difficult. J. A. Alexander urges us to see here the doing away of death itself. Only this understanding of death as used here does justice, he says, to the 'exquisite beauty of the passage, which the poet Burns, it is said, could not read without weeping.'

Through Christ God has brought salvation even from the power of death. And as John declares, in the new heavens and the new earth 'there shall be no more death.' God will complete his dealings with sin. Then we will indeed rejoice as we feast at his banquet in an even fuller sense. We will be forever assured that the one in whom we had boasted was indeed God. We will say,

> *Surely this is our God;*
> *we trusted in him, and he saved us.*

Perfect Peace

[*Isaiah 26:1–15*]

As chapter 25 concludes, we find that Moab has been laid low. It is as if her mountains are levelled. But upon

Judah, the mountain of the Lord, where he caused good to abound and to overflow, the hand of the Lord will rest in blessing.

In Isaiah 26 we have a song which Isaiah says is to be sung in Judah. He designed it to be sung antiphonally in thanksgiving to God after his deliverance of his people is accomplished. It is a song of praise for God's people in all ages, a song of praise for the peace he grants to his own.

Peace is a much sought-after commodity. Men search for personal peace. Efforts to bring about peace within a country are of pressing concern. Nations set up international organizations to seek to maintain peace on a world-wide scale.

But like many things such as happiness, peace is not something that you may obtain for the mere asking, something obtained in isolation. It is the fruit of other things such as understanding and humility. Peace, in its highest sense as Isaiah explains it in the chapter before us, is born of faith; it is for the righteous; it comes from God.

First, peace is born of faith. Peace belongs to the nation that keeps faith and to the person whose mind is steadfast. Such a nation or man trusts God. We are urged, therefore, to trust in the Lord forever. Peace is the fruit of faith.

Second, peace is for the righteous. God makes their path level, their way smooth. Walking in his laws, the righteous wait for him. Night and morning their desire is to him. To such, and to such alone, the Lord grants his peace.

Third, peace comes from God. As the righteous trust in him, God establishes peace for them. As in all else, so here: all that they accomplish he has done for them. He has cast out evil forces and enlarged his people. He has gained honor for himself and extended the borders of the land. He has established peace.

Peace has many facets. There is the peace which consists in the absence of friction and combat among peoples. There is the peace that glows with friendship and fellowship and unanimity. There is also the inward peace of the man whose mind is steadfast.

When Jesus declares that he is our peace he means it in all of these ways. He is breaking down the wall of partition and establishing peaceful relationships between Jew and Gentile. He is breaking down resentments and jealousies and competition among those who are his disciples. And he is, by his work on the cross, bridging the gap between a holy God and sinful human beings.

Jews according to the flesh have been greeting each other with *Shalom* for thousands of years. Even today in Jerusalem, tense with fear and noisy with the Muslim call to worship blasting away on the loud speakers, 'Shalom' is heard. But how vain and hollow it sounds from the lips of Jews who do not know the Messiah! Only the Jew or Gentile who has come to Christ understands 'Shalom' in the sense in which Isaiah uses it.

I had the privilege of being with my mother when, at the age of one hundred and one, she was waiting to be taken home. As I sang to her words of comfort at that hour I included one of her favorite gospel songs:

> *When peace, like a river, attendeth my way,*
> *When sorrows like sea billows roll;*
> *Whatever my lot, thou hast taught me to say,*
> *It is well, it is well with my soul.*

Mother could not respond in her weakness, but I knew it was well with her soul and I was confident that God was granting her peace. Perfect peace!

How will it be with you and me?

Birth to Her Dead

[*Isaiah 26:16–21*]

The American Negroes have loved to sing the story of Ezekiel and the dry bones and many of us have loved to hear their song. Ezekiel had a vision in the Valley of Dry Bones. There were bones on the floor of the valley and they were 'very dry.' At God's command Ezekiel told these bones to 'Hear the Word of the Lord.' The bones rattled and clattered, were arranged in order, and became human bodies. Then, at the breath of the Spirit of God, they came to life, just as the first man, when he was breathed upon by God's Spirit, came to life. These dry bones became living men; they stood up and made a vast army!

Verses 16 and 18 here have a ring of despair. The immediate reference is to the captivity, when Judah writhes and cries out in her pain. But then God promises deliverance when he comes out of his dwelling to punish the enemies of his people.

However, it is obvious that the reference goes much further than the captivity and deliverance in ancient Israel. From the time God promised Abraham that his seed would be as the sands of the sea for number, he had been renewing his promise that there would be a people raised up to his name from among the nations. We see that promise in this chapter. But God's people are aware of their weakness. Although they had some sense of mission to give birth to a people who would be God's people in all the world, yet thus far they had given birth only to the wind.

They needed verse 19 with its focus upon the power of God. No matter how weak God's people are in their mission, it is certain that his purposes will be accomplished. The earth *will* give birth to a people from among those who are now spiritually dead. Those who live in the dust are commanded to wake up and shout for joy! The dry bones are to hear the Word of the Lord and live. And it is the power not of men but of God that will accomplish this. It is his Spirit who will breathe into them and give life through Christ.

What an encouragement we find here for evangelism! We know, as Judah knew, that God has a people. We should know, as Judah should have known, that he will bring them to himself. Despite the weakness of the messenger, God blesses his message through his Spirit. Shame on us when we look at our weakness and do not count upon his power to bring nations to birth or dry bones to life!

There is further encouragement here for us as Christians. God will raise up our physical bodies. We do not restrict Isaiah's or Ezekiel's vision to the spiritually dead finding life in Christ and being given the new birth. We look beyond this to the day when Christ shall come and those who belong to him shall rise physically as he did. Paul writes in 1 Corinthians 15 about our perishable, weak, natural bodies that will one day be overcome by death. And he talks about imperishable, glorious bodies that will be raised up in power by God. That will be the ultimate of our experience, the consummation of Isaiah's declaration that God will swallow up death forever.

Sometimes we come to the Lord in distress, like Judah, barely able to whisper a prayer. God would have us 'wake up and shout for joy.' He would have us find strength in him as we hear the words of our Saviour to Martha of Bethany, 'I am the resurrection and the life. He who believes in me will live, even though he dies; and whoever lives and believes in me will never die' (John 11:25, 26).

'Do you believe this?' the Saviour asked Martha. And he asks us the same question.

Let Them Make Peace with Me

[Isaiah 27]

This chapter is a kind of gallery. God's fierce sword slays the serpent Leviathan. God carefully watches over his vineyard, ready to attack any marauder. God's Israel buds and blossoms and her fruit fills the world. Jacob casts off idolatry and experiences the full fruitage of the removal of sin. The city of the godless is desolated and finds no favour with God. And a trumpet sounds as God's people come from Assyria and Egypt to worship him in Zion.

As we attempt to distil these vignettes we see first a picture of the forces of unbelief. Leviathan was a great aquatic animal whose mention only in poetic passages may indicate that it is mythological. Leviathan here probably refers immediately to the Babylonian Empire, but it is representative of the fierce powers of the godless world. As we see, these powers will one day be destroyed.

Next we see God and his people as the vineyard keeper and the vineyard, just as we saw them sketched in Isaiah 5. There is the promise that Israel will flourish and that her fruit will nourish the whole earth. That this is a prophecy of the gospel age is confirmed when we compare it with Colossians 1:6, 'All over the world this gospel is producing fruit and growing, just as it has been doing among you since the day you heard it and understood God's grace in all its truth.'

And as we reach verse 12 we see that in that day the exiles from Assyria and Egypt will worship in the holy mountain in Jerusalem. How that harmonizes with God's blessing in chapter 19, verse 25: 'Blessed be Egypt my people, Assyria my handiwork, and Israel my inheritance'!

This is the way the Lord wants it to be. He will punish Leviathan, yes! But he would have men come and worship him in his holy mountain. Yes, he will march against those who confront him, if they persist. But he would rather have them come to him for refuge. He says,

> *Let them make peace with me,*
> *yes, let them make peace with me.*

Mankind is divided into those who are God's people and those who live in rebellion against him. The lines are drawn. But let us not pass by God's entreaty. He would rather *not* see any cast away. He calls out,

[95]

> *. . . let them come to me for refuge;*
> *let them make peace with me.*

In our zeal to proclaim a gospel that is by grace alone, let us not forget that it was grace that caused God to say these words. It is his love that prompts him to issue the 'whosoever will . . . ' And even as we recognize that God has declared a distinction between those who acknowledge him and those who do not know him, we need to say with loving entreaty to this hostile world around us: 'Make peace with God.' Paul said, 'We are therefore Christ's ambassadors, as though God were making his appeal through us. We implore you on Christ's behalf: Be reconciled to God' (2 Corinthians 5:20).

Who Is It He Is Trying to Teach?

[Isaiah 28:1–13]

As the Hawaiians honor visitors to their beautiful island with a lei[1] placed joyfully around their neck, so the ancients honored conquerors or heroes with wreaths of laurel or flowers which they placed upon their brows. This custom has been employed traditionally in competitions.

Isaiah speaks of two wreaths in this poem. The city of Samaria, set on a hill by Ephraim's fertile valley, is compared to a wreath. This city was glorious, the toast

[1]Wreath of flowers, leaves, etc.

of revelers. But it was very wicked, especially notorious for drunkenness. God, says Isaiah, has one who will lay that city low, even as hail and wind and driving rain destroy a floral wreath. We recognize this one whom God used against Samaria as Assyria.

The other wreath is God himself. The remnant of his people, after the apostate tribes have fallen, will rejoice in God as in a glorious crown. He will be a spirit of justice to the man who sits in judgment, a source of strength to those who turn back the battle at the gate. God will rest upon the head of this people as a crown of honor and blessing and glory.

With such a crown how can God's people dishonor him, staggering from wine and reeling from beer just like those in Ephraim? They are tipsy even as they see their visions and as they render decisions. How literally this reference to drunkenness in Judah is to be taken is a moot question. Surely the power of drink over Ephraim was very real and it would seem that there is more than a figurative meaning here with reference to Judah.

Whatever their particular sins, Judah is not wearing her crown, her God, honorably. She is not learning from him the lessons of his law by keeping his truth. His instruction down through the years has fallen upon deaf ears.

And yet Judah complains of God's reminders even while she ignores them. She complains of the prophet's methods of dealing with her. 'What kind of people does he think we are – children? Does he consider us too immature to be addressed once for all? Why does he have to repeat and repeat?'

But this is, truly, the way God – through Isaiah – sees fit to address them. He does it with great patience and longsuffering. God had approached the Israelites gently with promises of rest and repose, but they would not listen. So now he has to treat them like babies. And, in addition, he has to allow them to experience hurt as they fail their lessons! He has to allow them to be taught from foreign lips and to learn from enemy hordes what they refused to learn from their loving Covenant God. God will deliver his next lesson in the Assyrian language, Isaiah says.

Are we like babies who need the kind of teaching God had to give Judah? God is our crown. Because his Son wore a crown of thorns, we may wear as a crown our God himself. Do we wear our crown with dignity and responsible holy living? Do we learn the kind and gentle lessons God uses for our instruction? If not, we should not be surprised to find him using less palatable methods for our instruction. In what language will he deliver his next lesson to us?

Does the Farmer Plow Continually?

[Isaiah 28:14–29]

We are intrigued by the story of William Randolph Hearst, the newspaper magnate, publisher and editor, who attempted to remove from his home – and from his life – all reminders of death! He sought to make a covenant with death and the grave by ignoring it. But neither Hearst nor the rulers in Jerusalem could make a covenant with death nor an agreement with the grave. Such a covenant was with a lie which was considered a refuge and with false gods who were considered a hiding place. Hail will sweep away the refuge with the lie; water will overflow the hiding place, Isaiah says.

But there is one with whom we can make a covenant, one we can trust. And the man who trusts in him will never be dismayed. He is the precious cornerstone laid in Zion whom the apostles identified later in 1 Peter 2:6 and in Ephesians 2:20 as Jesus Christ. He is the head of the corner of the building which is the church of God. With him as our foundation and support we need not fear death. To us it is the beginning of an eternity with God.

God is building his church upon this cornerstone. But his work is not all constructive. Part of it has to be destructive as he punishes disobedience and unbelief. His tasks vary. They are alien, Isaiah says. His work is strange to us, but he does nothing without good reason. Of this we may be sure.

God is a farmer. As such he has many kinds of tasks, all needed for his work. Having a son-in-law who is a farmer, we are constantly amazed that a farmer has to know how to do such varied things and when to do them. The farmer does not plow continually or keep on breaking up and harrowing the soil all the year. After the soil is prepared he plants. And he does not plant and care for his crops each in the same way. He gives one kind of attention to the wheat and another to the soybeans. He harvests the corn and alfalfa[1] in different ways, too. Nor does he thresh endlessly. God teaches the farmer through experience, both his own and his father's before him. And God teaches him by the example of divine care over the children of men. Out of God's wonderful counsel and magnificent wisdom he teaches the farmer.

[1]A plant (with seed pods) grown for horses and cattle.

THE WELLS OF SALVATION

This was a song of encouragement and hope to Judah and it is the same to us. We rejoice that God does not break up the soil continually. We are glad that after the grinding of the grain he provides for the making of bread! To go back to an earlier figure, after the scourge and hail comes the laying of the tested stone in Zion to be the sure foundation for the one who trusts him.

Tucked away in this song of the farmer there is a special comfort for each of us individually. God, the prototype of all farmers, knows each of us personally and recognizes our specific needs. Some of us are rye and some are alfalfa. Some need one kind of care and some another. And God in his infinite knowledge and boundless love is concerned that each of us should thrive and bear much fruit. So he gives us what we need to this end.

Sometimes the way God plans for us may not be to our liking. But, as Martyn Lloyd-Jones says, God is concerned for our holiness more than for our happiness. He will bring this to pass. He will perfect that which concerns the people he loved so much that he sent his Son to save them.

He plows, but he does not plow continually.

'I Don't Know How to Read'

[*Isaiah 29:1–12*]

What was this vision of the City of David, called Ariel by the prophet? God would lay siege to the city and bring it low. The proud city would no longer speak forth in her glory. Her voice would come ghostlike from the ground where she would lie mourning and lamenting.

But then the city's many enemies – the way in which the prophet speaks seems to indicate that this prophecy is not of any specific, but of general nature – will themselves be turned back by God. He will come with all his might, with thunder and earthquake and wind and fire and will foil them. They will be as a dream, vanishing with the dawn. Or rather, they will be as a man who dreams that he was famishing and then is given food, only to wake up and find he is still hungry! The hordes of nations fighting against Zion might see her and crave her as a thirsty man craves drink, even dreaming that they have her in their possession, but no, God will snatch her away from them.

For Isaiah's fellow Jews this whole vision, he says, 'is nothing but words sealed in a scroll.' Ironically he comments that if the scroll is given to a man who *can* read, he will say he cannot read it because it is sealed; and if it is given to a man who *cannot* read he will say that he cannot read it because he doesn't know how to read. Isaiah is saying that God's people are spiritually blind and illiterate. He is saying, too, that men in any age grasp for any excuse for ignoring God's revelation.

We have seen this same thing repeatedly as we have been reading Isaiah together. God revealed himself and his plans for his people time after time. He showed them through the prophets his purposes for them, even for the City of David. But they did not respond to his revelation by waking up to the magnificent truths of his holiness and power. That is why he had to tell them 'here a little, there a little.' That is why he had to repeat. That is why he used so many different figures and approaches to drive home his teachings.

Yes, all of this is true, but there is more: 'The Lord has brought over you a deep sleep,' we read. It is in his inscrutable plan that these people have their eyes sealed. He is the one who has sealed the books, too. There would be a time when they would be opened, but that time had not yet come.

Calvin speaks concerning verse 10 in this way: 'As it belongs to him to give eyes to see, and to enlighten minds by the spirit of judgment and understanding, so he alone deprives us of all light, when he sees that by a wicked and depraved hatred of the truth we of our own accord wish for darkness. Accordingly, when men are blind, and especially in things so plain and obvious, we perceive his righteous judgment.' It is like the case of the sinners described in Romans 1 whom God gives over to their own sin as they prove their sinful bent by failing to glorify him in their lives.

The blindness and the stupor and the inability to read what was in the sealed books was all embraced in God's plan for history. It was brought about by man's own rebellion against the Maker and Revealer of truth. But it was, too, the plan of God that in Isaiah's day the mystery would still be hidden, which mystery would later be revealed in Christ. Though it was repeatedly brought to men's attention that the Messiah would usher in a worldwide kingdom of the Spirit, God did not see fit then to give men universally the ability to comprehend the divine revelation.

These things are difficult for us to understand. Isaiah will go on to deal with them in the rest of this chapter. But, for now, let us rejoice that the plan of our God included the eventual removal of the seals from the scroll!

The Deaf Will Hear the Words of the Scroll

[*Isaiah 29:13–24*]

Some of the Pharisees and teachers of the law came to Jesus with complaints about the disciples: 'They don't wash their hands before they eat!'

Jesus brushed off this complaint about his disciples for failing to adhere to the traditional ceremonial washing and took the opportunity to expose the sin of the questioners. They were nullifying the law of God for the sake of their own tradition. For example, they made gifts to God instead of using their money to help their needy parents, preferring to follow the *corban* rather than to obey by honoring their parents. Jesus quoted Isaiah 29:13 to them:

> *These people honor me with their lips,*
> *but their hearts are far from me.*
> *They worship me in vain;*
> *their teachings are but rules taught by men!*
> *(Matthew 15:8, 9)*

In every age, and in every land we find the same thing. Man in the pride of his own wisdom makes his own rules and lives by his own private philosophy rather than welcoming the wisdom of God into every department of his life. Nowhere is this tendency more flagrant than in the contemporary assertion that we need to 'do our own thing.'

Or man attempts to hide his plans from God, saying, 'Who sees us? Who will know?' He acts as though God did not make him, as though God knows nothing. This was surely true in Isaiah's day. We see it here.

But notice verse 18 where we find the familiar phrase *in that day*. With the coming of the Light of the World the gloom and darkness will be dispelled and the blind will see. Those who could not read will learn how to read. To change the figure, Jacob will no longer be ashamed when he sees the children God has raised up to him – spiritual children. These children will acknowledge the holiness of the God of their father and will stand in awe of him. This will be the gospel age. And the scroll will be unsealed.

And so it is! That is how it is that we, by the illumination of the Holy Spirit, may enter into the mysteries of God's scroll, understanding his plan for all the earth.

Revelation 5:9 and 10 speaks of a scroll, too, whose seals only the Lamb who was slain could break. Here the four living creatures and the twenty-four elders are singing a new song:

> *You are worthy to take the scroll*
> *and to open the seals,*
> *because you were slain,*
> *and with your blood you purchased men for God*
> *from every tribe and language and people and nation.*
> *You have made them to be a kingdom and priests*
> *   to serve our God,*
> *and they will reign on the earth.*

Here the children God raised up to Jacob – indeed, all creatures in heaven and on earth and under the earth and on the sea – are singing:

> *To him who sits on the throne and to the Lamb*
> *be praise and honor and glory and power,*
> *for ever and ever!*

> *Thank you, our Lord, for the Lamb who was slain. In*
> *him we gain understanding. From him we accept*
> *instruction, for he is worthy to open the seals of the scroll.*

'Stop Confronting Us With the Holy One of Israel'

[Isaiah 30:1–18]

After hearing a rather unsettling sermon, a lady in
one of our congregations, widow of a prominent
minister, offered my husband this bit of advice as she
left the church, 'My husband used to say, "Always send
the people away from church happy".'

Isaiah did not always send the people away happy.
But in his day as in ours this is what the people wanted.
Men say today to their ministers what they said in Israel
to their prophets:

> *Give us no more visions of what is right!*
> *Tell us pleasant things,*
> *prophesy illusions.*
> *Leave this way,*
> *get off this path,*
> *and stop confronting us*
> *with the Holy One of Israel!*

All over our country and world men and women are sitting comfortably in their pews listening to pleasant things, illusions. They are not being confronted with the Holy One of Israel.

And what will be the result? The sin of rejecting God's message – which is the sin of rejecting God himself – will become for them

> *Like a high wall, cracked and bulging,*
> *that collapses suddenly, in an instant.*

An architect friend of ours watched with chagrin while a retaining wall was being constructed along the edge of a pavement on a property where, high on the hill, a large office building was being built. His expertise warned him of the danger of using this particular method of construction for a wall probably twenty-five feet high that would be supporting such weight. A couple of days after Bill shared with us his concern, we drove down the street and found the wall collapsed, its beautiful grey stones scattered over the pavement and out into the street! The rejection of God's truth could not have been more forcefully portrayed for modern man than by this figure.

God offers salvation in repentance and rest, in quietness and trust, but men will have none of it. They want to act according to their own wisdom. Judah wanted to seek help from Egypt, from Rahab the Do-Nothing, as Isaiah called her! And such an alliance would not bring help or advantage but rather shame and disgrace. God longs to be gracious to men, to show them compassion. But modern men, like Judah, will have none of it. They are rebellious, deceitful children, unwilling to listen to God's unbending Word.

Christians, is this sometimes the case with us? Ask to be confronted with the Holy One of Israel! Ask for the truth. Do not always want to hear your pastor speak of pleasant things. Ask for visions of what is right. If the man in the pew demands God's truth from the pulpit, a new day will dawn for the world's churches.

When the Lord Binds Up the Bruises

[Isaiah 30:19–33]

Countless Christians have been touched by the testimony of Joni Eareckson Tada. Joni was a popular and talented young girl who excelled in sports. She was a fine horsewoman and swimmer until one day in a diving accident she suddenly lost the use of arms and legs. She became a paraplegic! All of her personal hopes and dreams were shattered in a second.

Joni went through the classic stages of shock and disbelief, of rebellion and depression that a person typically experiences in grief. But through all of her trials she learned acceptance and even joy in knowing that 'the Lord binds up the bruises of his people and heals the wound he inflicted.' Today Joni is a well-known artist, using her mouth to hold her brush or pen. She has appeared in a film telling her story. She has addressed audiences of thousands of people. She has made a recording of songs which are her testimony. And she heads a thriving organization which ministers to persons who, like herself, are handicapped in one way or another.

In Joni's books, *Joni* and *One Step Further*, she lays bare her heart, describing the conflicts she has experienced with an intensity few know. But loudly and clearly from the pages comes her testimony that although the Lord gave her the bread of adversity to eat and the water of affliction to drink, he was there with her himself! And through the days and months and now years of living with this handicap Joni has heard God's voice behind her, saying, 'This is the way; walk in it.' She has seen the pride of self, which she had known as a girl, become to her as a defiled thing and has said to it, 'Away with you.'

Primarily Isaiah has been speaking of national calamity in this chapter, chiefly calamity stemming from the onslaughts of the Assyrians. Now he holds out to Jerusalem a hope. He reminds his people of God's character, of his grace, his presence and his guidance. He declares to them the return after captivity. And, as so often is the case, he would have them see across the centuries the gospel age.

But, although Isaiah's emphasis is on the national level, the tenderness here revealed makes portions of this chapter particularly precious to those undergoing personal affliction and bereavement. Do you see in verse 26 a nurse, bathing a wound ever so carefully and then bandaging it skilfully and gently?

Joni rejoices in the comfort of knowing that it is, indeed, the Lord who gives us this bread of adversity, that it is he who inflicts these wounds upon us. This is, after all, the supreme comfort in time of trouble for those who know they can trust the One whose love caused him to send his own Son for their sake! This truth makes us sing. It causes our hearts to rejoice as men rejoiced on their way up to the temple on a day of holy festival, playing their flutes in glorious praise to God.

As a Lion Growls

[*Isaiah 31*]

Judah, with many hills, was not a land whose people had a large cavalry. Egypt, however, with her flat terrain, offered excellent facilities for developing a cavalry and was noted for her fine horses. But the horses of Egypt were flesh, not spirit. And as Judah relied on Egypt both she and Egypt would fall. For the power Judah needed was power that God alone could provide, the God who is spirit and truth. And Judah had forgotten the song of David which said:

> *Some trust in chariots and some in horses,*
> *but we trust in the name of the Lord our God.*
> *They are brought to their knees and fall,*
> *but we rise up and stand firm (Psalm 20:7, 8).*

Isaiah would have Judah be fully aware of God's power to protect her. He would have her see how feeble the Egyptians and all others are to render her help. The prophet pictures God as a great lion astride his prey. A band of shepherds have come at the summons of the one whose sheep has been snatched away. But the mighty lion standing over the sheep glowers at the shepherds and defies their shouts and clamor. Just so will God do battle on Mount Zion, protecting his people against their enemies.

To change the figure, God will be like a mother bird hovering above her fledglings in the nest, protecting them against every harm. He will shield his people and rescue them.

The term *pass over* in verse 5 appears in quotation marks in the NIV. The translators imply that it is borrowed from the scene in Egypt when the angel of death passed over the homes of the Jews who had sprinkled the blood of a lamb on the lintels of their doors. God had given to his people in Egypt his protection, through the promised Christ, against the angel of death who would bring death to pass upon the firstborn of all the houses of Egypt. So now would he shield Judah. And so will he shield and deliver us. The blood of the Lamb of God is sprinkled on the lintel of the church today so that death's angel will not visit her.

One day, Isaiah says to Judah, you will know God's sovereign power and will reject the idols your hands have fashioned. Some day you will see the frailty of the nations, even of Assyria, before the Lord. Why not do it now? 'Return to him you have so greatly revolted against.'

Those who have seen a mother bird protecting her young can appreciate the figure of the bird hovering overhead ready to spring into action. But when we consider the power of Satan and his angels which is so evident all around us, perhaps the figure of the lion is even more comforting. The Lion of the Tribe of Judah, so gentle with his own people, is not frightened by the shouts of his adversaries and will protect us against them. How much we need to be reminded of his sovereign power!

Quietness and Confidence For Ever

[*Isaiah 32*]

God considers it so important that men see the evil effects of sin and the beautiful fruit of righteousness that he approaches these subjects from many angles in the book of Isaiah. In this chapter he begins by telling of a King who will reign in righteousness and as he concludes the chapter he comes out with the wonderful statement that the effect of righteousness will be quietness and confidence for ever. Righteousness is the theme of the whole chapter. In fact, literally, verse 1 can be translated in a most emphatic way: 'According to righteousness will there reign a king.'

The first stanza is probably the inspiration for the familiar gospel hymn:

> *Jesus is a rock in a weary land,*
> *A shelter in the time of storm.*

In this hymn we feel utmost security, quiet orderliness and satisfaction, all stemming from King Jesus who reigns in righteousness. All of this is blessed truth.

Many, however, including the translators of the NIV, believe that the subject of the verb *to be* in the second verse is *each man* rather than *he* (which would refer back to *a King*). Each man will be like a shelter and refuge from the wind and storm; like streams in the desert; and like the shadow of a cliff in a thirsty land. This may shock us at first, but we see in it the power of the great King who changes men and enables them to be strong in him and to strengthen others. This interpretation accords with Christ's promise that when the Holy Spirit would come his disciples would do greater things than they had seen him do.

In the second stanza Isaiah elaborates upon this change in men in the coming kingdom. There will be enlightenment and discernment. This will affect the behavior of men as well as their minds and speech. It will affect the regard with which they hold others, so that fools will be known for what they really are and will not be called noble. But the truly noble man will be completely characterized by nobility! Divine wisdom will pervade that kingdom.

Isaiah breaks off from his description of the coming kingdom to warn Judah of present complacency. He warns men as well as women who feel secure to hear what he has to say and to shudder and tremble. Their assumption is that everything will continue as it now is. They virtually say, 'We are doing quite well, thank you, without any help from God or man.' The captivity is ahead and he warns them of it.

But the prophet returns to the theme of righteousness. The Spirit will be poured out on God's people from on high, he says. Then

> *Justice will dwell in the desert*
> *and righteousness live in the fertile field.*
> *The fruit of righteousness will be peace;*
> *the effect of righteousness will be quietness and*
> *confidence for ever.*

Although their city is levelled completely, and although, we may say, all material things have been stripped from them, Judah will be blessed. The material and spiritual blend so naturally that this had to come through to Isaiah's contemporaries as a promise of return from captivity. Did they perceive in it, as we surely do, a description of the kingdom of our Lord Jesus?

As these words are being written, Lebanon is a battlefield for the nations, the Poles are struggling valiantly for their freedom, and all the earth dreads a nuclear holocaust. What promise is more fitting in this world of turmoil and fear than the promise of quietness and confidence forever? And from what alone can this peace stem? From righteousness! Ultimately only by serving the King who reigns in righteousness shall we have quietness and confidence forever.

The Sure Foundation for Your Times

[Isaiah 33:1–16]

We have observed young people who have cast off parental authority and fled into a communal life come to the point of formulating their own rules in order to survive. We have seen other young people who have left their family home, ostensibly to be rid of the control of an authoritarian father, become affiliated with a group which is under the thumb of a guru who dominates all of their life.

Human beings have a built-in need for structure and routine. They have, although many of them deny it, a basic need to have their limits defined. They need, in the tumult of their souls, to be able to hear a voice saying – as the seas hear it saying,

> . . . *This far you may come and no farther;*
> *here is where your proud waves halt*
> (*Job 38:11*).

The Lord does not promise a Zion where each man will be living according to his own desires, a society in which there is no certainty as to what is going on and who is in charge. He promises a Zion where he himself will be 'the sure foundation' for 'their times'.

This sovereign Lord is not unaware of the needs of his people. He will grant salvation and wisdom and knowledge to them. His is a reign in which there is an increasing awareness on the part of the ruled ones of the principles under which the rule is exerted and a growing understanding of the truths by which their king governs. His people will grow in their perception of his will. The fear of the Lord will be the key to this treasure that they will possess in him.

The beautiful fifth and sixth verses where we read this are placed in the midst of words of distress and pleas to God for his gracious help. Isaiah, as spokesman for Judah, longs for God. In verse 2 he prays that God will be their salvation in the time of trouble. He recognizes the power of his God before whose voice of thunder the peoples flee.

This is a forlorn picture, with brave men crying in the streets and envoys of peace weeping bitterly. Now the streets are deserted.

The Lord speaks. He calls upon these peoples to acknowledge his power. Hearing him, the sinners in Zion are terrified, knowing they cannot live in the presence of a God who is a consuming fire. But those who walk righteously and live by God's law dwell on the heights. Their refuge is the mountain fortress. Their God supplies their needs.

He will be a sure foundation for their times.

The Lord Jesus told a story of two men. One built his house upon the sand and watched in dismay when the rains and floods came and undermined it – much as certain Californians in the spring of 1983 watched their homes collapse under the rains and the raging Pacific tides. The other man built his house upon the rock and it stood through all the storm. As we listen to the words of God and live them we are building upon him who is a sure foundation at a time when 'houses' built upon shifting sands come to ruin.

As we see the basis of morality and security eroding all about us, we thank you, our God, for the assurance that our refuge is a mountain fortress and that we dwell on the heights.

The King in His Beauty

[*Isaiah 33:17–24*]

Isaiah's contemporaries are made to look beyond the captivity to their return to Jerusalem, where they will see a king of their own again on the throne. They will think back upon the days of their travail. They will marvel that the chief officer, the one who took the revenue, and the officer in charge of the towers, are gone! They will hardly be able to believe that those proud people whose language was foreign to them are no longer their oppressors.

Now their beloved city will be peaceful, a tent whose stakes will never again be pulled up. Their Lord will be there in his might, granting her peace. Though now they are a ship ill-prepared for action, in that day things will be different. Zion will enjoy plenty to the full. There will be health and there will be forgiveness of sin.

In true Isaianic fashion the material and spiritual are blended. And there is the familiar mingling, too, of reference to the post-captivity days of Judah and days of the new heavens and the new earth. Only when the heavenly King returns in glory will Zion experience peace without any disruptions of sin. Only then will there be permanent assurance that no enemy will sail her broad rivers. Only then will everyone in Zion be free from illness.

In that day will we ponder the former terrors? Will we marvel that those who, often blatantly, worked against the church, the Christian school and the family are gone? Those arrogant people who now exert such influence in the legislature, the media, in education, science and the arts, adopting a purely humanistic orientation and speaking a language foreign to the Christian, will no longer be there!

The day that is yet to be defies description. Ears have not heard and eyes have not seen, nor has it entered into the thoughts of men, what that day will be. But we need desperately to perceive the extent to which this prophecy is already being fulfilled in our midst. For the Lord is *today* our judge and lawgiver. He is our Saviour and those who dwell in his Kingdom have been forgiven. And we have the promise that the stakes of our church will never be pulled up. The gates of hell will not prevail against her.

> *Forgive us, our Lord, when we are so farsighted that we fail to see about us the peaceful abode which is your church here and now. Help us to rejoice in the present reign of our King in his beauty, a reign over a land that indeed stretches far. Help us to rejoice that the sins of those who dwell in that land are indeed forgiven.*

To Uphold Zion's Cause

[Isaiah 34]

Here is a chapter, like some others, that may make us want to say, Why, Lord? How useless! How cruel!

When we looked at Isaiah 13 we considered God's utter, moral right to do with his creatures whatever he wills. We spoke of his holiness and abhorrence of sin. We spoke of his union with his people which compelled him to put down their enemies. And we spoke of the necessity for the power of evil to be restrained.

Today as we read Isaiah 34 we are struck with a solitary phrase against the otherwise unexplained manifestations of God's anger and declaration of vengeance – TO UPHOLD ZION'S CAUSE. This purpose of God is related to those we have mentioned. But there is a new quality here. God's purpose is not simply to support the people of Zion, but the system, the laws and the purposes basic to their way of life. Zion's cause, which God does everything necessary to uphold, is simply *the truth*. Even if blood must be shed, the truth must be upheld.

In order to bring home the point of today's consideration let us look at the perils of peace. As the author of Ecclesiastes says, there is a time when war is appropriate as well as a time for peace. There are times when peace is insidious!

Peace is insidious when I smile and tell myself that the nagging sin within me is not really serious; when a wife does not admit her failure to support her husband's leadership; when a husband does not risk opposition in the household by gathering wife and children around God's Word; when a child does not ask his parents the questions about faith that are plaguing him.

Peace is insidious when the congregation does not confront the pastor with his lack of emphasis upon God's law. Or when the pastor does not preach on the sin of covetousness.

Peace is insidious when the citizen does not object to having abortions funded from his tax monies, or when the staff of the state obey in silence a Führer who is murdering thousands of Jews.

Peace is insidious – when to speak in the vernacular – we refuse to rock the boat.

There *is* a time for war and for protest. There is a time for opening up a sore with a knife. When the right time to take action has come is sometimes quite evident. Sometimes it is difficult for us to determine. But our God knows when it is time to break the peace of the nations to uphold the cause of Zion. He knows when peace is insidious and the day of retribution has come.

We need not be embarrassed or apologetic about upholding Zion's cause. True, we are fallible and need to exercise discretion. But sometimes the Christian virtues of submissiveness and gentleness must give way to the contrasted virtues of courage and straightforwardness and to holy boldness. When God's truth is maligned we cannot sit idly by in acquiescence.

For the sake of Zion the line of the Messiah had to be preserved – even if this meant the destruction of nations. To uphold Zion's cause God found it necessary to give up his own Son to the death of the cross.

Your God Will Come

[Isaiah 35]

> *Crocus – spearing the snow,*
> *Proudly raising her purple flag,*
> *Claiming the world for Spring.*

After a long, cold Maine winter, this bright little flower surely brings encouragement! Isaiah experienced its cheer in his day and land, too.

In his artistry Isaiah knew we needed chapter 35 after chapter 34. It renews us to read again of Judah's rejoicing in God's sunlight, his spring. 'Your God will come,' the prophet promises. Judah was a desert, a parched land, a wilderness. She will be glad and rejoice. She will burst into bloom like the crocus. She will shout for joy. She will see 'the glory of the Lord, the splendor of our God'.

[119]

The people of God, whose hands have grown feeble, whose knees have given way, and whose hearts have become fearful, are being encouraged. Isaiah says to them:

> *Be strong, do not fear;*
> *your God will come,*
> *he will come with vengeance;*
> *with divine retribution*
> *he will come to save you.*

Your God will come! It is Jesus, God come in the flesh, who will open the eyes of the blind and unstop the ears of the deaf. With the coming of God's Son the whole earth will begin to experience release from the curse brought upon it by the sin of Eden. Romans 8:21 makes it abundantly clear to us that eventually this release will be complete. '. . . The creation itself will be liberated from its bondage to decay and brought into the glorious freedom of the children of God.' Ever since Satan's defeat at the cross the promise of Genesis 3:15 has been in process of fulfilment. The tide has turned and the healing is being accomplished. Every spring we have a symbol of the ultimate fulfilment of God's promise.

With our Lord's coming again in triumph the transformation will be complete! And there will be a special highway, the Way of Holiness, reserved for the redeemed, the ransomed of the Lord, the people of the Way. On it they will enter Zion singing. Everlasting joy and gladness will overtake them. And sorrow and sighing will flee away.

'Amen. Come, Lord Jesus.' (Revelation 22:20).

On Whom Are You Depending?

[Isaiah 36]

It is interesting to observe that chapters 36 through to 39 are predominantly written in prose. These chapters form a historical interlude connecting the first and final major parts of the book of Isaiah. Chapters 36 and 37 are connected with the first part of Isaiah, relating the attempt and failure of Sennacherib to destroy God's kingdom. Chapters 38 and 39 are related to the final section of the book and tell of the godly Hezekiah and the Babylonian exile to come.

Looking at chapter 36 we see that Sennacherib asked a good question. He sent his field commander to the palace administrator, the secretary and the recorder and questioned them: 'On whom are you basing this confidence of yours . . . On whom are you depending?'

Were they depending on their own strategy and military strength? Sennacherib scorned that dependence. What about Egypt? The field commander calls Egypt 'a splintered reed of a staff, which pierces a man's hand and wounds him if he leans on it.'

'And if you say,' the brazen Assyrian hurls out at them, '"We are depending on the Lord our God", isn't he the one you have neglected?' They had neglected God, yes, but here the Assyrian shows his ignorance of Hebrew religion by interpreting the removal of high places and altars by Hezekiah as an indication of neglect of God.

Hezekiah's chief men were intimidated by the emissary of the world conqueror. They requested him not to speak in Hebrew because the people listening on the wall would understand and be alarmed. 'Speak to us in Aramaic,' they pleaded, 'then we can understand you, but they cannot.'

Defiantly the commander again spoke loudly in Hebrew. He warned the people not to be deceived by King Hezekiah into thinking that God would deliver them from the Assyrians. He invited them to go with Sennacherib back to Assyria where, he said, they would have peace.

No gods have delivered their people from Assyria, he reminded them. How can Jehovah do it?

In obedience to Hezekiah the people remained silent. Then the palace administrator, the secretary and the recorder tore their clothes to express their grief and went to Hezekiah with the day's experience weighing heavily upon them.

The story of Isaiah is clear. But the man who does not even appear in this part of the account is the one who stands out most distinctly – King Hezekiah! Surely his faith is what the chapter is all about. His faith was quite evident to the people sitting on the wall obeying him with their silence. Shocked they were, shaken and grieved. But the faith of their king was an example which sustained them. If he could depend upon the Lord God in this time of trouble, so could they!

And so can we.

He . . . Spread It Out before the Lord

[Isaiah 37:1–20]

We, who have found Jesus our matchless friend and refuge, admit to our shame the accusation of the gospel song:

> *O what peace we often forfeit,*
> *O what needless pain we bear,*
> *All because we do not carry*
> *Everything to God in prayer!*

When the three men, Eliakim, Shebna, and Joah, came with torn clothing to tell Hezekiah the news of the threats of the King of Assyria, the king went to the temple of the Lord. Where else could a man of God go at a time of crisis? He sent men to Isaiah with a message, 'This day is a day of distress and rebuke and disgrace, as when children come to the point of birth and there is no strength to deliver them.' He added, 'Maybe God will hear the words of the field commander spoken in ridicule and will rebuke him. Therefore, pray for the remnant that still survives.'

Isaiah answered him that the Lord would frustrate the plans of Sennacherib and that he would flee to his own country. There he would be killed. Hezekiah did not need to know the details. God encouraged him with the promise of Sennacherib's flight.

Soon after that, Sennacherib heard a report that the king of Cush was marching out against him. This prompted him to try to get things settled with Judah quickly. So he sent a messenger to Hezekiah with a letter advising him not to let the 'god' he was depending on deceive him. He warned Hezekiah of the fate of other nations whom Assyria had overthrown despite their gods.

What did Hezekiah do at this crisis? He went to the temple of the Lord. He took the letter from Sennacherib's messenger and spread it out before the Lord. And he prayed. Earnestly he prayed. Hezekiah knew that his God was not like the gods Sennacherib had quite easily thrown into the fire and burned. He knew his God was the Almighty Creator and Lord over all the kingdoms of the earth. His prayer was for protection, yes, but also for the glory of his God, that all nations would know that he alone is God. This was his dependence. This was his faith.

> *O Lord, how often when problems come to us we worry and fret! How much needless pain we suffer because we do not take our burdens and spread them out before you! We are grateful to Joseph Scriven who over a century ago[1] taught the church to sing about your Son, our burden-bearer. We are grateful to Paul who taught Christians the same lesson nearly 2,000 years ago, 'Do not be anxious about anything, but in everything, by prayer and petition, with thanksgiving, present your requests to God' (Philippians 4:6). And we are grateful to Hezekiah who preached an action sermon from this text some 600 years before Paul! Cause us, we pray, to heed the lesson you have been teaching your people for so many years.*

[1]Probably about 1855. His hymn begins, 'What a Friend we have in Jesus'.

Because You Have Prayed

[Isaiah 37:21–38]

Hezekiah prayed. God, Creator and Sovereign of the earth, was moved by this man's prayer. Because he prayed God spoke words of calamity against Sennacherib. And he brought them to pass. We mentioned the story in connection with Isaiah 14. God sent his angel to slay 185,000 men in the Assyrian camp. So the king of Assyria broke camp and withdrew from before Jerusalem to Nineveh and stayed there. One day some years later, when he was kneeling in the temple before his god Nisroch, two of his sons cut him down with a sword. And another son, Esarhaddon, succeeded him on the throne.

Sennacherib's insults had been against the Holy One of Israel, not simply against Jerusalem. Now, in the song of the Lord concerning him, the Virgin Daughter of Zion tosses her head in scorn at a king without an army returning to his homeland.

Isaiah has Sennacherib giving a catalog of his own victories. Then there is a simple but staggering statement:

> *Have you not heard?*
> *Long ago I ordained it.*
> *In the days of old I planned it;*
> *now I have brought it to pass.*

So God is speaking to Sennacherib:

'You were able to destroy these nations, yes, but only because this was my plan. I am in control of events, not you.' And now (as Sovereign)

I will put my hook in your nose
and my bit in your mouth,
And I will make you return by the way you came . . .

Sennacherib will not, says God, enter the city of Jerusalem.

God's sovereignty, his foreordaining all things that come to pass, was not a doctrine concocted by the Protestant Reformers, or even by Paul. Where could it be set forth any more plainly than here in Isaiah?

So simply and unashamedly this sovereignty stands next to the faith of Hezekiah! 'Because you have prayed to me . . ,'God says, 'I have preserved Jerusalem from Sennacherib.' And then he says, 'Long ago I ordained it.' God ordained the safety of his people before time began. For his own sake and for the sake of David he ordained it. For the sake of his Son, the son of David.

Hezekiah's prayer and God's eternal purpose stand side by side. God is not embarrassed to have them so close together. Isaiah is not embarrassed by it either. Why should you and I feel uncomfortable and struggle to reconcile prayer and God's sovereignty? We may leave in his province the harmonizing of the two. And then we, like Hezekiah, may come confidently to our God in prayer.

All My Sins behind Your Back

[Isaiah 38]

As commentators read verse 6 here, where God promises to deliver his people from the king of Assyria, they conclude that this chapter is probably a flashback, taking us prior to the events described in chapters 36 and 37. Let us bear this in mind as we examine this chapter which has received so much attention.

Some readers call Hezekiah weak and fretful: he had been strong in faith but now he wept as he pleaded with God to prolong his life. Others are sceptical of the whole account as they struggle with the phenomenon of the shadow cast by the sun turning back. Still others excitedly attempt to prove from scientific history that at one time the sun did turn back.

But let not the reader involve himself with such matters to the extent of missing something really more significant. This is the 'writing of Hezekiah after his illness and recovery.' More significant than the psychology of his weeping, or even the science of the movement of the sun, is the theology of the good king's message in this passage.

Hezekiah had been at the point of death. But he recognized that it was indeed God who was 'cutting him off from the loom'. And in his distress he looked to heaven and prayed, 'O Lord, come to my aid.' The Lord touched his body and prolonged his life. To a

God who can turn back the course of death in the life of a man, turning back the course of the sun is no problem.

As Hezekiah now looked back upon the period of his illness he was humbled. He said,

> *I will walk humbly all my years*
> *because of this anguish of my soul.*
> *Lord, by such things men live;*
> *and my spirit finds life in them too.*

He recognized that his suffering was for his own benefit. He believed that, in part at least, he was spared to praise God, since in the grave men cannot praise him. So in the extended life the Lord gave him he purposed to praise God and to tell his children about God's faithfulness. He purposed to sing all the days of his life in God's temple.

His praises would be of the two-fold salvation of God. He would sing of how God in his love had kept him from death. He would sing of how God had put all his sins behind his back. 'The Lord will save me,' he declared.

Surrounded by all the comforts of health some three millenia later we may be inclined to call Hezekiah a coward. God would rather have us see in this chapter the divine power to halt the process of death, to turn the course of the sun, and, more significantly for us, even to grant sinful man salvation. He would have us see his love, who plants in the anguished soul a song of rejoicing in the finding of life!

Peace and Security in My Lifetime

[Isaiah 39]

Was it pride or naiveté that caused Hezekiah to show to the envoys from Babylon what was in his storehouse – the silver, the gold, the spices, the fine oil, his entire armory and everything found in his treasures? Did he give praise to his God for all these blessings? God has not chosen to tell us these things.

Nor can we be sure that the report of Hezekiah's wealth precipitated the Babylonian captivity, because this had been planned and even attempted before. But from our vantage-point the inspection tour seems a very unwise act. And God spoke to Hezekiah through Isaiah foretelling the carrying away to Babylon of these very riches Hezekiah had shown the men, as well as the capturing of some of the king's own family that would come after him.

And what do we make of Hezekiah's reply? God's word is good? Yes, God's word, no matter what it is or how it affects us, is good. Amen. So be it. But Hezekiah appears to be saying, 'It is good because the evil will not affect me personally, even though it affects my family. At least while I am alive things will be all right'. Perhaps, after all, this speech harmonizes with the turning-his-face-to-the-wall scene. Perhaps Hezekiah did have a streak of cowardice.

But we must watch our judging. In an area and era of so much distress and bloodshed is it not understandable that a man would rejoice in the prospect of a little pocket of peace? Hezekiah knew how his people had disobeyed God. He knew God's righteous judgment was imminent. A few years of respite would be most welcome!

And furthermore, who are we to cast blame on him, we who are, as a nation, clasping to ourselves peace and security in our lifetime? As Francis Schaeffer points out, just as long as we have personal peace and freedom and a measure of security in our days, we imagine that all is well! We are not concerned that our peace and freedom and security might not last into the lifetime of our children and their children. We are not concerned that our peace and freedom and security might even be at the expense of those who come after us. We are not concerned that as we pollute our world and misuse its resources we are robbing or even killing our children. We are not bothered by the pile of intolerable debts they will have to pay. We are not troubled enough that social engineering is materializing before our eyes into a flood that threatens to sweep away all traces of dignity and freedom bestowed upon the man God created. Let him who has no guilt cast the first stone at Hezekiah!

Just so we have peace and security in our lifetime . . .

O Lord, we who may be calling Hezekiah a coward may some day be called the same by those who come after us. Forgive us! And help us to follow the example of this man as we spread before you the problems of our day. Help us, like him whose example of faith moved his people to resist the words of Sennacherib, to be a model for those who are being lulled into sinful complacency.

Comfort My People

[Isaiah 40:1–11]

Following his historical interlude, written in prose, Isaiah embarks here upon the final and precious concluding section of his prophecy. Here are some of the most beautiful passages in the literature of the world, inspired by God's Spirit and written by a Jew of the eighth century B.C. for all succeeding generations of mankind to cherish.

Chapter 40 does not begin a new book. This section was not written by another Isaiah. The whole book from chapter 1 through to chapter 66, is one harmonious whole. The themes of the earlier chapters are the themes of the later chapters. Jesus himself credits Isaiah with the authorship of passages in the earlier section as well as in the later. But it is as though, after laying a solid, broad foundation, Isaiah is now ready to bring forth in glorious triumph the full, clear message of the Messiah and the gospel age he is ushering in. The gospel of grace is unfolded in greater detail. It is as though Isaiah were now pulling out all the stops!

God tells Isaiah to comfort his people. He wants them to be comforted by his promises. Later he would send them the Comforter. He wants them spoken to tenderly as a loving shepherd whispers to the little lamb he carries close to his heart. Later he would send them the Good Shepherd.

And what is the message of comfort they receive?

God's Word is sure! Though men may be cut down as grass or flowers of the field, God's Word will endure. And just as sure is the coming of the Lord. In the earlier sections Judah's sins had been catalogued; they had been described thoroughly. When the Lord comes, the provision will be made for dealing with these sins. The atonement, which is brought forth so clearly in chapter 53, is here in capsule where we read that the sin of God's people 'has been paid for'.

Isaiah brings the comfort of the anticipated end of earthly captivity. But this is a mere shadow and suggestion of the comfort of the loosing from spiritual captivity at the advent of the Son of God and the coming of his kingdom.

God would make preparation for the coming of his Son. The mountains will be made low and the valleys raised, we read, and the rough places will be made level. Nothing is to hinder his coming. As we think of the early settlers in our own country struggling to ford rivers and cross mountains in their westward trek across the American continent, and then think of the valleys now filled in and the mountains now levelled or tunneled through to accommodate super-highways, we have a graphic picture of the way preparation was made for the glory of the Lord to be revealed among men.

As part of this preparation God would send a herald, the man we call John the Baptist, to preach repentance of sin and to call men's attention to what God was doing. Verses 3 to 5 here are applied to John specifically in Luke 3:4–6.

God has come as he promised to do. The glory of the Lord has been revealed. Lift up your voice, God says, do not be afraid. Say to the cities of Judah – to the cities of the world, 'Here is your God!' Are we lifting up our voices with a shout?

Isaiah blends the sovereignty of God with the love and comfort of God in these verses. And, indeed, if he were not sovereign, what would his comfort be worth? If he did not deal tenderly, what comfort would his sovereignty afford? As we proclaim God's message let us be careful to blend, as Isaiah did, all of the facets of the character of God so that men may indeed participate in the true comfort he offers.

To Whom Will You Compare Me?

[Isaiah 40:12–26]

How do you describe God? To whom can you compare him? Some four hundred godly ministers and students of the Bible met for five years, 1643 to 1648, at Westminster Abbey in London to attempt to summarize and crystallize the teachings of God's Word. They struggled long over many questions, one of them being, Who is God? Finally, prayerfully, they came up with a magnificent answer from the Scripture: 'God is a Spirit, infinite, eternal and unchangeable, in his being, wisdom, power, holiness, justice, goodness and truth.'[1] This statement has become a classic summation of the doctrine of God.

All the attributes of God which these devout scholars brought together in this statement are written large in

[1]This is the answer to 'What is God?' (Question 4) in *The Shorter Catechism*.

the Gospel according to Isaiah, many in this fortieth chapter. In words inspired by God's Spirit and couched in sublime poetry, Isaiah reaches us in a way the Westminster divines cannot do. Not only does he satisfy our minds; he satisfies our hearts.

Let us select a few of the characteristics of God from the *Westminster Shorter Catechism* to see just how Isaiah treats them in this chapter:

Spirit. As Isaiah describes the idols of men, fashioned of gold and silver and wood, he gives us a new sense of what it really means to have a God who is a living, personal Spirit. To accommodate himself to our understanding, God describes himself in human terms. But he is not like the gods of the heathen, he is a Spirit. He is not confined in a wooden image, in one locality, in one age. He is not mere stuff, matter. He is a Spirit!

Infinite. Isaiah enlarges our concept of infinity as he sweeps along in splendid rhetorical questions:

> *Who has measured the waters in the hollow of*
> *his hand?*
> *or with the breadth of his hand marked off*
> *the heavens?*
> *Who has held the dust of the earth in a basket,*
> *or weighed the mountains on the scales*
> *and the hills in a balance?*

Isaiah does not confine himself to earthly metaphor. He takes us into space and challenges us to see the heavens being measured by the breadth of a hand! Our God is infinite.

Eternal. We perceive anew the significance of a God who existed before time began as we read verse 26. Isaiah points us to the heavens which God created and to the starry host which to its Maker is so familiar that he has a name for each heavenly body. He is the Alpha and the Omega. He is outside of time.

Wisdom. Isaiah did not know about the universe what the modern scientist knows. But he knew what many modern scientists are ignorant of. He knew the One who made it and the One who holds it together. He knew the One who decided it should be the way it is and the rules by which it should operate. He asks:

> *Who has understood the Spirit of the Lord,*
> *or instructed him as his counsellor:*
> *Whom did the Lord consult to enlighten him,*
> *and who taught him the right way?*
> *Who was it that taught him knowledge*
> *or showed him the path of understanding?*

Our God is infinite in his wisdom.

Power. The God of Isaiah is not merely a mastermind. He is a God who acts. He knows how to plan a world, yes, but he knows also how to bring into being what he has planned and to supply it with energy for its operation. The power of God awes us as we read of how he stretched out the starry firmament for a canopy over the earth. And how he brings princes to naught and rulers of the earth to nothing,

> *. . . no sooner do they take root in the ground,*
> *than he blows on them and they wither,*
> *and a whirlwind sweeps them away like chaff.*

Thank you, O our great God, for who you are! Thank you for enabling men through the ages to systematize your truth for our greater comprehension. Thank you for feeding our spirits by the poet Isaiah. Thank you for your

[135]

*Holy Spirit who causes us to perceive who you are and to
respond to you through your Son.*

On Wings Like Eagles

[*Isaiah 40:27–31*]

Kefa Sempangi, prominent Ugandan professor,
preacher and public servant, has written a book, *A
Distant Grief*. As he describes the atrocities of the ruler
Amin he points out that there is a boundary beyond
which human beings cannot comprehend the evil in this
world. 'Beyond that,' he says, 'everything is a senseless
chasm. It is here in a nightmare of utter chaos that
human feeling dies. It is here, where death and terror
seem to have full dominion, that even the deepest of
human sorrows becomes but a distant grief.'

Sempangi makes the parallel between this and the
boundary 'beyond which human beings cannot comprehend the glory of God.' As we were reading
yesterday in Isaiah 40 we might have been feeling that
we were out beyond our depth. Here was a God who is a
Spirit, wrapped in infinity, eternity, wisdom and power
all too far away, too high above us – a distant glory.

But the being of our God is not exhausted in these
attributes. And Isaiah brings God down to us – or
rather, lifts us up to him – in these concluding verses.

When we consider a God before whom we are like
grasshoppers, we may well say, My problems and
frailties are not known to him. He pays no attention to

them. But Isaiah explains to us that our everlasting Creator, God, has an understanding beyond our comprehension. He understands not only the workings of his stars and his volcanoes; he understands the workings of our minds and hearts. He understands you and me and cares for us in our own particular weaknesses and troubles.

The Lord is strong and his strength enables him to endure. His strength, furthermore, is communicable. To those whose hope is in him he will give his strength and he will increase their power. When they are weary and weak, when they stumble and fall, he will renew their strength.

As I write these lines, there is a fierce storm whipping up the sea outside my window. Trees bend over. But with calm strength the sea-gull remains poised in mid-air, oblivious, it would seem, to the force of the elements. God will give those who trust in him wings like an eagle and enable them to rise above the storms.

We have a son who completed the San Francisco marathon. He explains how, at about the 20–mile mark, he was *finished*. Beyond that, sheer force of will kept him going through the motions to the end. God will give to those who trust him the strength to run and not be weary.

And what about the lackluster daily walk that all of us find so fatiguing? God will give his people power to walk and not to faint.

God is all that Isaiah paints him earlier in this chapter. But, oh, how thankful we are that he is, too, a God who is touched by our infirmities and who enables us to endure the hardships of this life. How thankful we are that the poet speaks not chiefly of the physical strain and weariness. He speaks of the struggles of the soul:

the spiritual exhaustion, the discouragement, the stress of waiting, the inertia – all of the maladies of the soul to which men have been subject since the fall.

How thankful we are that God is love. He is a God who loves. He loved us so much that he gave his Son to come and live as one of us, experiencing in his own body and soul the tiredness and weariness common to human life.

Yes, God understands. That is precisely why he knows how much we need to hear about the wings of an eagle.

Be Silent . . . and Speak

[Isaiah 41:1–16]

'Be silent before me, you islands! Let the nations renew their strength! Let them come forward and speak.' How do we explain this apparent contradiction from the lips of a God who cannot contradict himself?

God, before whom the nations of the world are like a drop in the bucket, is worthy of the utmost respect. He enjoins respectful silence upon the nations which, like Assyria, taunt him. And, when a people recognizes who he is, the only appropriate response is silence. Read in Job 40:4 and 5 the words of the chastened Job,

> *I am unworthy – how can I reply to you?*
> *I put my hand over my mouth.*
> *I spoke once, but I have no answer –*
> *twice, but I will say no more!*

The parent, who also deserves respect because of his authority under God, can relate to these words. The child who talks back does not show honor to his parent; nor the student to his teacher. Silence is the appropriate response to the Sovereign God as the guilty sinner stands in his presence.

What does God mean, then, when he says, 'Come forward and speak'? Notice the phrase in between: 'Let the nations renew their strength.' As we look back to chapter 40, verse 31, we read, 'Those who hope in the Lord will renew their strength.' God invites men to hope in him, to have faith in him. As they do so, their strength is renewed. As they look to him with faith in his Son they are no longer in the place of the guilty sinner but are in his sight forgiven sinners – saints. Now they are invited to speak!

But this speaking will not be with the taunts which he had silenced. This speaking will be with confession, supplication, praise, addressed to the God whose sovereignty is at last recognized.

God's working in the nations is evident. Men see it and tremble. It is as though they had been attempting to cheer one another by saying, 'Be strong,' while at the same time they were making gods of their own. They were making gods which they called *good* but which needed to be nailed down so that they would not, like Dagon, topple over! Their gods had no strength. To whisper '*Be strong*' to their fellows was but to whistle in the dark. God's promise to those who look to him is reliable. In him who renews strength, men can rest. A man encourages his brother in this God with a '*Be strong*' that has real meaning!

This is the world picture: a general manifestation of God's power; a fear on the part of men, yet a stubborn clinging to impotent, man-made ideologies; a desire on the part of God that the nations recognize him and come to him; a general invitation to men to return to their Creator.

Out of the nations of the earth God has chosen Israel or Jacob, descendants of his friend Abraham, to be a people for himself. And the church today is God's Israel. From the nations of the earth Christ is building his church.

Israel is God's servant and God is Israel's God. Isaiah describes here this covenantal master-servant relationship. The servant owes obedience to his master and receives love and protection from him in the face of enemies. He whose master is strong does not need to fear. Is not our master God Almighty?

We, his chosen ones, have been silenced before our God. We have seen his holiness and stood before him in awe. We have looked to him in faith and have been strengthened. Let us now come forward and speak!

Tell Us What the Future Holds

[Isaiah 41:17–29]

Men have been trying to know the future ever since Eden. And there have always been some who have been ready to predict it. In Eden Satan spoke to our first parents about the future. A soothsayer told King Saul about events to come.

In Deuteronomy 18:22 we read that if the prediction of a prophet comes true we will know that this prophet is from God. This is God's own test of a true prophet. There are many false prophets whose predictions are ambiguous or who are particularly astute guessers. Even the printed predictions tucked in the Chinese fortune cookies that we get at the restaurant sometimes turn out to be amazingly accurate! But a consistently successful prophet has to be sent from God himself.

Here God challenges the false gods. He asks the idols to predict future events. He asks why they never foretold the mighty deeds of men which he brought about in his governing of the nations. He says:

> *Who told of this from the beginning, so that we*
> *could know,*
> *or beforehand, so that we could say*
> *'He was right'?*
> *No one told of this,*
> *no one foretold it,*
> *no one heard any words from you.*

'See, they are all false', God concludes. 'Their deeds amount to nothing; their images are but wind and confusion'.

In this we see, too, why God does foretell the future. It is a confirmation of his truth, his reality, his omniscience, his control over history. As his prophecies come true, men can say, See, it is as he said. Surely, he it is who is God. He is the one who planned it all and so it came to pass as he foretold. Fulfilled prophecy has been a confirmation to God's people through the centuries that theirs is the one true God and that he has spoken.

And so it is today. The gods men serve cannot save them. They cannot give them peace and love. They fail to do anything. There is nothing but wind and confusion in them.

We know this. Do we confront our neighbors with it and point them to him to whom all is laid bare, past, present and future? Men look to the stars – even in this scientific, 'enlightened' day – to learn the future. Do we point them to him who made the stars?

He Will Not Be Discouraged

[*Isaiah 42:1–13*]

In Isaiah 41:8 God called Israel his servant whom he had chosen. So Israel was. And so, too, the church, the Israel of God, is today God's servant.

But God speaks here in this chapter of a certain individual, not a nation. He says,

> *Here is my servant whom I uphold,*
> *my chosen one in whom I delight.*

Here God foretells the advent of his Son who is to come to earth in the form of a man, in the form of a servant. Quietly, unobtrusively, he will come, without the fanfare accompanying the birth of the son of a king, even the birth of a son to Prince Charles and Princess Diana. Matthew 12:18–21 tells us of the Lord Jesus and his fulfilment of these words of Isaiah. In his gentleness

Jesus considered the weak in faith. In his faithfulness he spoke justly.

Isaiah goes on:

> *He will not falter or be discouraged*
> *till he establishes justice on earth.*
> *In his law the islands will put their hope.*

His work will be ongoing. Through the years he will not falter or be discouraged. The seven churches of Asia will need to be chided roughly for their failure to conform to his will. And through hundreds, yes, thousands of years, other churches will need similar chiding. But he will not falter or be discouraged.

How is it that God's servant has not faltered and is not discouraged? Because of the certainty of the accomplishment of the task. He *will* establish justice on earth, Isaiah tells us. In his law the islands *will* put their hope. God has said it. What he foretold with reference to the coming of the Messiah took place. Jesus did come. This further fulfilment will come to pass also. The servant will bring all of God's people to their knees before the Creator.

Read how the prophet Isaiah expresses it:

> *See, the former things have taken place,*
> *and new things I declare;*
> *before they spring into being*
> *I announce them to you.*

New things I declare? Yes, the wonder, the mystery of the worldwide kingdom that the Lord Jesus would establish. That is the new thing. And in verse 10 Isaiah tells the people to give thanks for this new thing. He tells them to sing a new song.

In the Psalms we read of the new song, too. It is to be the song of all the earth. In Revelation 14:3 we hear the redeemed from the earth actually singing this new song. And the lyric is given us in Revelation 5:9 and 10:

> *You are worthy to take the scroll*
> *and to open its seals,*
> *because you were slain,*
> *and with your blood you purchased men for God*
> *from every tribe and language and people*
>   *and nation.*
> *You have made them to be a kingdom and*
>   *priests*
> *to serve our God,*
> *and they will reign on the earth.*

Today as we look around we may be discouraged as we see the humanist elite gaining increasing influence in the media, in education and the arts, and in science. We may be discouraged as we see God's people fragmented, indifferent, frightened. We may wonder whether the kingdom of God has indeed come.

Not so the Son! 'The servant' is encouraged by the certainty of the words of the Father. He hears men and women even now in this corner of the earth and that, singing a new song. And he knows that one day the vast combined chorus for which they are practising will sing it before the throne of God!

Look, You Blind, and See

[*Isaiah 42:14–25*]

Many times in the Old Testament reference is made to the days in the future when God's people would see. We understand that this refers to the gospel age when the Holy Spirit would come and spiritual insight would be granted in a new and more abundant way. We rejoice to be alive in this day of greater privilege. And we look forward to another day when, with the abolishing of all sin, we shall see things even more clearly.

But in today's reading God tells his people that, even in the eighth century B.C., they should be *seeing*. Their blindness is, in part at least, due to their own refusal to see. And remember, these were people who were living in the Valley of Vision. You will want to read again Isaiah 22:1–14 to get this whole picture.

God says that he will lead the blind by paths they have not known. He calls the blind and deaf to see and hear. He is saying that nothing is wrong with their eyes or ears. Who, he asks, is blind and deaf but his servant who has seen and heard many things but has paid no attention to them? The trouble is with the heart.

We must pause a moment over the word *servant* as Isaiah uses it here. The reference is obviously no longer to the Lord Jesus, as it was in the beginning of this chapter. Isaiah is reverting to the use of the word which he employed previously in Isaiah 41:8 ff. to refer to the chosen people, Jacob. You will find that the prophet uses the word 'Jacob' in verse 14 of the same chapter. Jacob has sinned, he says, and will not follow God's ways.

God's servant Jacob is a people who have seen many things. They have seen God's law, great and glorious. They have seen their Creator God in the worlds he has made. 'The heavens declare the glory of God,' one of their poets had taught them to sing (Psalm 19:1). They have seen his faithfulness as he delivered them from Egypt, from the sea, the wilderness, the enemies around. And they have seen in prospect his glory that will come – the kingdom his Son will usher in and the final victory over all.

But they have paid little attention to what they have seen. They have heard little though their ears have been open. Because

> . . . *they would not follow his ways;*
> *they did not obey his law.*

So he handed them over to plunderers. His burning anger, the violence of war

> . . . *enveloped them in flames, yet they did not*
> *understand;*
> *it consumed them, but they did not take it to heart.*

Are we blind and deaf, we who possess the completed revelation of the Lord Jesus and God's Holy Spirit to apply his truths to our hearts? Do we who have such privilege pay attention? Do we obey God's law? What about *our* hearts? Much more than Isaiah's compatriots we are called upon to see and to hear and to act upon our knowledge. How much do we have to suffer at the loving hand of the Lord before we take his words to heart?

Called by My Name

[Isaiah 43:1–7]

What glorious words we find in the seventh verse of this passage – 'called by my name'! How greatly they would encourage the hope that God would bring his people Israel back to Jerusalem after their captivity! But they are even more significant as an encouragement to us concerning the building of Christ's church. 'You are mine,' God says. 'You are precious and honored in my sight . . . I love you.'

Christ told his disciples that he had others who were not of their fold. He would bring them to himself. They too are called by his name.

Picture the believing Eskimo whom God created and formed and called by his name. He belongs to God and God acknowledges him as his own. He is brought from the north. 'Give him up,' says God; 'he is my son.' God has redeemed him.

Picture the swarthy woman from the South Sea Isles, created by God and called by his name. She is God's adopted child. She is brought from the South. 'Do not hold her back,' God says; 'she is my daughter.'

Prison doors open. God's children whom he has created and formed and called by his own name come forth from their bondage to sin. He is with them. They are precious and honored in his sight. He loves them.

The true wife delights to be called by the name of her husband. The bride, which is Israel, the church, delights to be called by the name of the Bridegroom, the Lord Jesus Christ. Think what it means to be called by the name of your Creator and Redeemer. A man takes a risk in allowing a woman to bear his name. She might dishonor it by low or disgraceful behavior. God's work is never at risk. He knows us altogether. And yet he is willing to say, 'You are mine.' What condescension! What grace!

The disciples were called *Christians* first at Antioch. Ever since Antioch they have been called by Christ's name. We cringe at the blasphemous use of the word *Christian* in the Middle East and elsewhere merely to differentiate from Jew or Muslim. Some day it may prove costly – here where we live – to be called by the name of the Saviour. Even today men and women are passing through the waters and walking through the fire in some parts of the world as they did in the past, simply because they bear the name of Christ.

To such people God says, 'Do not fear.' And they have the confidence and security that he who so loved them will, in his infinite power, keep them safe for eternity. He is with them. They are called by his name.

You Are My Witnesses

[Isaiah 43:8–21]

Jesus was not inaugurating some completely new thing when he spoke to his disciples assembled in Jerusalem after his resurrection. When he said to them, as we read in Acts 1, 'You will be my witnesses,' he was not using unprecedented language. He was expanding upon an old principle enunciated here in Isaiah. He was fulfilling prophecy.

God's people in the eighth century B.C. had heard these words from the mouth of God:

> All the nations gather together . . .
> Let them bring in their witnesses to prove they
>   were right,
> so that others may hear and say, 'It is true'.

Isaiah puts it ironically. Of course the things the heathen were saying were not true.

Jehovah it was, not the heathen, who told of things before they took place. We have read this in Isaiah before. No one could bear witness that the proclamations of the idols were true. Jehovah alone revealed, redeemed and proclaimed. In his hands alone are the makings of history. And his people are his witnesses.

A witness tells what he knows. The word comes from the Old English *witan* meaning *to know*. How much do we know? What we know we must tell.

[149]

In a sense, we are witnesses whether we tell anything or not. If we who are called by his name do not tell what we know of God, then we are poor witnesses. By our very silence we are saying that what we know is of little significance. We are saying that our God is not worth talking about, that he is not as important as the baseball players or the recipes we talk about so often – or the weather!

What have we seen that we should tell? We have seen the promised one of David's line come to his people. 'It is true,' as the prophet foretold it. God it is who brought this to pass. We have seen come to pass these very prophecies of God through Isaiah concerning the spread of the gospel through the Gentile world. They were true words, proclaiming that their author is the true God. And we have seen ourselves, lost in sin, brought to the feet of this One, lifted up by him, given a new mind, a new life. 'It is true.'

What he had said came to pass in the accomplishment of the redemption which had been promised centuries before and in the application of this redemption to our own lives. This we have to tell. By word and life we have to tell our family and our neighbors – even our world – that God is God.

We know. We are his witnesses. And we, his chosen people whom he formed for himself, are to proclaim his praises!

I Remember Your Sins No More

[Isaiah 43:22–44:5]

Have you ever thought you had really forgiven someone and then awakened one morning to find the same bitterness still there nagging at you? Have you been assured of the forgiveness of a friend for something you had done against him, but found that you could not forgive yourself for the heartache you had caused him? Have you ever said, 'I can forgive, but I cannot forget?'

We all need to take lessons in forgiveness from God. In Christ he has forgiven his people. Our sins he has put behind his back. He has buried them in the depths of the sea. He remembers them against us no more.

As we are forgiven, so should we forgive. And so *can* we forgive through his strength. Our lives must not be embittered by grudges held against others. Since we are forgiven we must and can forgive and forget.

We empathize with Peter asking the Lord how many times we must forgive. But let us not forget the story Jesus told him about forgiveness. A certain king ordered that one of his servants and his family be sold for the payment of a debt. The servant's pleas were heeded and the king cancelled the debt and let him go. The debt was several million dollars in our currency.

The forgiven servant went out and found a man who owed him a few dollars. He grabbed him and began to choke him, demanding that this debt be paid. When the debtor pleaded with him for forgiveness he refused to grant it, throwing the man into prison until he could repay.

The king was informed of this incident and called his forgiven servant back. He confronted him with his sin and had him put in jail until he should repay all he owed.

The words of Jesus to Peter are awesome: 'This is how my heavenly Father will treat each of you unless you forgive your brother from the heart' (Matthew 18:35).

Our first father sinned. Our representative rebelled against God. We ourselves have burdened God with our sins and wearied him with our offences. We deserve disgrace, scorn and destruction. 'The wages of sin is death' (Romans 6:23). God would be justified in paying us the wages we have earned.

But we can argue with God! We can remind him that he blotted out our transgressions and remembers our sins no more, for the sake of his Son. We can confess that we sinned in Adam. We can acknowledge that it was our sin that sent his Son to the cross. We can confess how we have to this day wearied him with our sin, how we have failed to forgive our fellows. But then we can claim the forgiveness provided through his Son.

And he will indeed forgive and bless. 'He will pour waters on the thirsty land and streams on the dry ground.' He will pour his Spirit on his people and on their children. This is his promise.

Men will be happy, Isaiah says, to claim the name of God; they will rejoice to belong to him. Before Christ there were means provided for Gentiles to enter the family of Israel and to take the name of Jehovah. Now, all over the world, Jews and Gentiles alike are coming to

Christ for forgiveness. In the face of disinheritance and disdain Jews are acknowledging that truly Christ is the Messiah who was to come. And they are taking his name. Christians are springing up like grass in the meadow. Like poplar trees they are growing up by the flowing streams.

God has forgiven them and he remembers their sin no more. He, the Holy One of Israel, in whom there is neither darkness nor shadow of turning, has forgiven Jew and Gentile the sins that separated them from a Holy God – for the sake of his Son!

> *O Lord, our model, as we look to you, may we learn what forgiveness is.*

No One Stops to Think

[*Isaiah 44:6–20*]

The writers of the Scriptures are fond of pointing out the folly of worshiping a god of one's own making, but no chapter of the Bible presents idolatry with more telling irony than this chapter. How graphically are described the blindness and ignorance of the man who shapes a god and casts an idol which is nothing!

In fine detail Isaiah tells how the blacksmith and the carpenter go about their work. He describes how part of a tree is used to make a god while another part is used to warm the carpenter and to bake his bread and roast his meat. A stick of wood is worshiped with a prayer, 'Save me; you are my god.'

Men who worship such gods know nothing and understand nothing; their eyes are plastered over so they cannot see and their minds are closed so they cannot understand. They do not give time to examine the folly and shame of worshipping something that is less intelligent and less powerful than they are. Their deluded hearts mislead them so that they do not recognize that their idol, the product of their own hands, is a lie. It is nothing.

In more enlightened days and cultures men still fail to give time to examine the folly and shame of worshiping a god which is less intelligent and less powerful than they are. Whether the product of a man's hand – the home, the boat, the empire – or the product of his mind – the private theology or philosophy – this idol *has* to be a lesser thing than he is. The things he treasures are worthless. But no one stops to think.

But we must go one step further. Even man himself, the god of the humanist, cannot be a fit object of worship. The God who made man and who taught him all the truth he has known has to be greater than man. God alone is worthy of his worship.

The concept of creatorship is basic in man's thinking. As men turn from the glorious fact of Genesis 1:1 they become blind and embrace a lie rather than the truth. Back in 1929 D. M. S. Watson, President of the Zoological Section of the British Association for the Advancement of Science, made this significant statement: 'The theory of evolution was a theory universally accepted, not because it could be proved to be true, but because the only alternative, special creation, was clearly incredible.' Unwilling to accept God's Word, men turned to falsehood and carried with them millions of others who did not stop to think.

The Christian never needs to be ashamed when others imagine his beliefs to be intellectually indefensible. The inspired author tells us this in Psalm 119:99:

> *I have more insight than all my teachers,*
> *for I meditate on your statutes.*

And this is the case with all who have God for their mentor. The humble disciple or learner at the feet of Jesus knows better how to think, as did Mary of Bethany, than does the unbeliever with a long string of degrees after his name.

Men do not turn from God because they have become too well educated. They fail to embrace him because they are not educated well enough. They do not stop to think. In fact, with darkened intellects they cannot think truly. Only when the Holy Spirit renews their minds, and all things become new, can they think truly.

O Lord, be our mentor. Help us to see you as Creator. Help us to conform all our thoughts and practices to your truth. Fill us with the knowledge of your will through all spiritual wisdom and understanding in Christ. Help us to know him whom to know aright is life eternal.

I Have Redeemed You

[Isaiah 44:21–28]

A small boy made a boat which he loved very much. One day as he was sailing it on a stream it slipped away from him and was lost. Later the boy saw his boat in a store window. He took his precious savings to buy back the boat. As he held it close to himself he said to it lovingly, 'You are twice mine. You are mine because I made you, and you are mine because I bought you.'

We cherish the application of this story. We are God's because he made us and we are his because he bought us back. This is the meaning of redemption. Adam sinned and man was estranged from his Creator and Father, becoming a child of Satan. At the cross God bought him back with the price of the blood of his only Son.

It was not an idol of wood or stone, it was not some ideology, some wealth or worldly power that saved Israel, or that can save any man. The Lord Jehovah himself is Jacob's Redeemer and the Redeemer of all who belong to his Son. 'I have redeemed you,' said God.

Recently we watched the mist hanging low in the lush Napa Valley in California. Now it veiled the hills. Now it was gone. God has swept away the sins of his people like a cloud, their sins like the morning mist. He has displayed his glory in them. He calls upon the heavens and the earth to bear testimony to this redemption and to sing for joy, and shout and burst into song.

God describes how the redemption of Israel will be manifested. He promises that the towns of Judah will be rebuilt and that Jerusalem will again be inhabited. He even names Cyrus the Mede as his shepherd who will accomplish what God pleases for Jacob. Through him this rebuilding will be accomplished as an accompaniment and illustration of salvation.

And he is describing, too, the greater redemption of his people by the death of his own Son whom he will send. With what a cost did he buy back his children whom he had made!

'Return to me', God says. 'I have redeemed you'. Surely this places our salvation in its true light. It all issues from God, the God of grace. He did not redeem us or save us *because* we had returned to him or because he knew we would *decide* to return to him. It was because of his own good pleasure that he redeemed us. Humbly we stand before him. And with the heavens we sing for joy at his glorious redemption:

> *For the Lord has redeemed Jacob,*
> *he displays his glory in Israel.*

Though You Do Not Acknowledge Me

[Isaiah 45:1–13]

At the conclusion of the forty-fourth chapter we saw a specific statement concerning Cyrus, an historical character not born probably until 120 or 140 years after Isaiah's death. God called him 'my shepherd,' indicating that this heathen king of Persia would gather God's people like sheep and bring them back to their own land. Cyrus would even see that Jerusalem was rebuilt and the foundations of the temple which Nebuchadnezzar had destroyed would be laid for rebuilding.

In the present chapter God speaks further about Cyrus, his anointed. This term *anointed* was used with reference to prophets, kings and priests, as well as to Christ who holds all three offices. Christ's very title Messiah means the *anointed one*. To be anointed is to be

set aside and equipped by God for a special task. God
will take hold of the right hand of Cyrus to subdue
nations and to open gates before him. For the sake of
Israel he will do it. He will do it, too, so that Cyrus – and
indeed all men from the rising of the sun to its going
down – will know that God the Lord does all these
things and that there is no other God.

It is a matter of history that in 539 B.C. Cyrus
conquered the Babylonians who had been holding the
people of God captive for seventy years. In Ezra 1:1–4
we read that in the first year of his reign, 'in order to
fulfil the word of the Lord spoken by Jeremiah, the
Lord moved the heart of Cyrus king of Persia to make a
proclamation' concerning mobilizing the Jews in
captivity for their return and the rebuilding of their
temple.

The people made their preparations. Cyrus brought
out from the heathen temples the articles which had
been taken from the temple of God in Jerusalem by
Nebuchadnezzar. The treasurer of Cyrus made an
inventory of these treasures which we may read in
Ezra 1. The people received these things and returned
with them to their beloved city where they rebuilt the
temple.

As we place side by side the prophecies of the return
under Cyrus and the historical account concerning its
fulfilment we cannot but say, HOW GREAT IS OUR
GOD! Indeed, it is as he has said. He alone foretells and
it comes to pass. He alone is Lord.

But perhaps the strangest feature of this prophecy
and its fulfilment is that Cyrus was an unbelieving
Gentile ruler. The God of Israel called him by name and
bestowed upon him a title and honor though he did not
acknowledge him as God. The phrase is repeated:

> *I will strengthen you,*
> *though you have not acknowledged me.*

Even in his unbelief, as he learned of God's prophecy concerning himself, Cyrus consciously fulfilled it. What more specific evidence could we find of the worldwide scope of the power of our God than this? Not only does he use in the furtherance of his cause those who acknowledge him, but he sets aside a Cyrus for a special work in the execution of his divine plan for history. He involves a man who does not acknowledge him in setting the stage for the sending of his Son to redeem his people Israel, his Son who is *the* Anointed One.

We need to be reminded today that God is using world leaders for his purpose whether or not they acknowledge Him. He is God over all!

There Is No Other

[*Isaiah 45:14–25*]

We recently had the pleasure of a long conversation with a learned Jew of fine character. He was searching for the truth about the Messiah and requested our prayers for him in his search. The wife of this gentleman is a professing Christian, a Gentile. But she wants to believe that there must be some way other than through Christ for him to be saved. A Jew as kind and gentle as her husband, she tells herself, could not be turned away by the God of the Old Testament.

But there is no other way. There is one God, the Creator of all things and the One before whom history is unfolded. He knows the beginning from the end. And he is sovereign over creation and history. Even the unbelieving King Cyrus of Persia, as we saw at the beginning of this chapter, was bent to the purposes of this one God. Even Cyrus, who did not know him truly!

Look at the fourteenth verse where the tall Sabeans take up the refrain:

> *Surely God is with you, and there is no other;*
> *there is no other god.*

The Lord himself echoes it:

> *I am the Lord,*
> *and there is no other.*

As we turn to the New Testament we read in Philippians 2:10 and 11 from Paul's sketch of the life of the Lord Jesus:

> *At the name of Jesus every knee should bow,*
> *in heaven and on earth and under the earth,*
> *and every tongue confess that Jesus Christ is Lord,*
> *to the glory of God the Father.*

In this context Paul uses the theme from Isaiah 45:23 to apply to God Incarnate. Notice the similar phrases:

> *Before me every knee will bow;*
> *by me every tongue will swear.*

Before this one God Jew and Gentile alike need to bow the knee. They need to turn to him to be saved. And he has come in the person of his Son who said, 'I am the way and the truth and the life. No one comes to the Father except through me' (John 14:6).

It was Jews to whom the Jew Peter made the sweeping statement given us in Acts 4:12, 'Salvation is found in no one else, for there is no other name under heaven given to men by which we must be saved.' Our Jewish friend and his wife together may come to the Father only in the name of his Son. There is no other way.

How we rejoice in that way! How we love to sing the song of Christina Rossetti as we bow our knee before him:

> *None other Lamb, none other Name,*
> *None other Hope in heav'n or earth or sea,*
> *None other Hiding-place from guilt and shame,*
> *None beside thee!*

I Will Carry You

[Isaiah 46]

There is a story of an older man who had a dream. In his dream, all his life was laid out before him. He saw it as a long path on which were the imprints of two pairs of feet walking side by side. But as he looked at it carefully he had a problem.

He said to the Lord, 'I see your footprints beside mine along all of my life's path. But why, O Lord, when I came to the hard places in life, did you leave?'

The Lord answered him. 'True, when you came to the hard places there was only one pair of footprints. Those, my son, are my footprints. When the way was too difficult for you, I did not leave you. I picked you up and carried you.'

This chapter is about a God who carries his people. Not only does God remind us that he is our Creator and that he has carried us from birth, he goes on to promise that he will continue to carry us –

> *Even to your old age and grey hairs*
> *I am he, I am he who will sustain you.*
> *I have made you and I will carry you.*

We may have before us a time when weakness will require others to carry us physically. There may come a time when we will need to be sustained because of weakness of spirit. Our heavenly Father will carry us. What a promise!

In the ninth verse God tells those who remain of the house of Israel to remember former things, those of long ago. He tells them that his purpose will stand. And he declares that what he has planned he will do. He says:

> *I am bringing my righteousness near . . .*
> *I will grant salvation to Zion.*

He loves his people and they can depend on him as their support for all their days.

Who can say this but our God Jehovah? The people of Babylonia have no gods like him. They have to carry their gods. Their gods cannot carry them. A god of the heathen, though it be made of precious silver or gold, must be transported on men's shoulders. When it is set in its place, there it stands. From that spot it cannot move. O yes, one such god moved! Dagon moved. When the ark of Jehovah was taken into the temple of Dagon in Ashdod, Dagon fell to the ground on his face before the ark. He had to be put back in his place (1 Samuel 5).

There are those who prefer to consider themselves above dependence upon any religious 'crutch'. In their arrogance and self-sufficiency they prefer to think that they can handle their lives without the help of God or man. This is the spirit of the age. And we see its consequences in the wrecked lives all around us.

Not so the child of God!

Perhaps you have seen a young child walking down the street hand-in-hand with his father. Suddenly he stops and turns to his father with arms upraised. His confident voice pleads simply, 'Carry!' How good to have a Father to whom we can look, confident though weary, and say, 'Carry!'

I Will Continue For Ever

[*Isaiah 47*]

Often we read in Isaiah the glorious refrain, 'I am the Lord; there is no other.' A beautiful, true, majestic refrain it is. Now those words become hollow and cheap and blasphemous. They have been taken by Babylon and applied to herself. Babylon is made by the skilful poet to say, 'I will continue for ever – the eternal queen.' She, whom Isaiah calls a wanton creature, lounging in her security, says of herself, 'I am, and there is none besides me.'

In irony Isaiah speaks to the city which men everywhere fear. She will be shamed. She will sit on the ground in dust, without a throne. No longer will she be called queen of kingdoms. God, in his anger at the rebellion of his people, had given them into her hand, but in pride and cruelty Babylon went further than she should have done, showing no mercy to them. Now she will fall. She who said she would never come to grief will suffer the loss of children and husband. A catastrophe she could never foresee will suddenly come upon her.

Babylon had received counsel from her astrologers who made monthly predictions. She had consulted sorcerers. But these, like an idol dropped overboard from a Chinese junk, could not save themselves. Of course they could not save her.

Babylon, who boasted she would continue forever, fell. As we noticed earlier, the Book of Revelation speaks about Babylon, too. Note chapter 18, verse 21: 'Then a mighty angel picked up a boulder the size of a large millstone and threw it into the sea, and said,

.   *With such violence*
the great city Babylon will be thrown down,
never to be found again.'

Babylon is a type of any nation which has 'shed the blood of prophets and of saints and of all who have been killed on the earth.' Babylon is any country which takes the words that apply to God and applies them to herself. Babylon is any people who say, 'I will continue for ever – the eternal queen . . . I am, and there is none besides me.'

What people is exempt from this guilt? The United States? Great Britain? Only the true Israel of God, guilty but by grace forgiven, can say, 'I will continue for

ever.' Only she, as the Bride of God's Son, is the eternal
queen.

Leave Babylon

[Isaiah 48]

Israel was dull and stubborn, worse than the oxen
Isaiah pictured in chapter one. Over and over God has
had to remind these people of their Creator, the one
who called them as a nation and redeemed them. He has
had to call to their memory his prophecies of the future
and their fulfilment. In this chapter he rebukes them
again for their recalcitrance. He says:

> *The sinews of your neck were iron,*
> *Your forehead was bronze.*

But the Jews have been refined and tested in the
furnace of affliction. Now they will be brought out of
captivity. Persia's Cyrus, 'the Lord's chosen ally', will
overcome Babylon and will set the Jews free to return to
their home land.

So God says to Israel:

> *Leave Babylon,*
> *flee from the Babylonians!*
> *Announce this with shouts of joy*
> *and proclaim it.*
> *Send it out to the ends of the earth;*
> *say, 'The Lord has redeemed his servant Jacob.'*

You have heard the term *secret believer*. You have known people, perhaps more commonly today than at other times, who claim to be Christians but admit no need to confess Christ publicly and unite with his people in the organized church. Even in countries where it is safe to make open acknowledgment of Christ you find them, satisfied, perhaps, with the electronic church but living day by day in Babylon. And you find people in the church on the Lord's Day who have not left Babylon.

Isaiah speaks to such. There is a double message in verse 20 for his people: leave Babylon and proclaim your redemption. How well this dovetails with the double message to Christians found in the New Testament: come out from among them and confess Christ before men.

God in his anointed Son, to whom Cyrus points forward, has released us from sins's captivity. Surely we will not be content to remain in bondage! We will leave Babylon. And surely, then, the least we can do is to proclaim our release and our Saviour with joy in order that others may know. We will send to the ends of the earth the proclamation, 'The Lord has redeemed his servant Jacob!'

This is the Lord

> *who teaches you what is best for you,*
> *who directs you in the way you should go.*

As we leave Babylon and follow him our peace is like a river and our righteousness is like the waves of the sea. So the Lord blesses those who heed the commands of their Redeemer.

Before I Was Born

[Isaiah 49: 1–13]

In very recent years there has been wide discussion concerning when human life begins. Does it begin at birth? at viability? at conception? The morality of abortion hinges upon the answer to this question.

God's Word, which is consistent in its answer, speaks to this issue here in Isaiah 49. Human life begins *at least* at conception. We may in a certain sense trace its beginning to the mind of God before creation, but we cannot say that it begins later than conception.

The Lord has made mention of my name from my birth. But he also called *me* (the pronoun indicates a *person*, not a *thing*) before I was born. He formed *me* in the womb. I was not a blob, a p.o.c. (product of conception) during those months of my pre-natal development. I was a human being.

This chapter, though, however clearly it brings out this tremendous fact about the history of the individual human being, embraces a larger concept. The Lord made me to be a particular, special human being – or, in this instance, he made his people to be a particular, special people – even before birth! The Lord made Israel to be his servant, in whom he would display his splendor.

Gracefully, Isaiah moves to the Messiah, the epitome of servanthood, and we find that we are in the midst of a beautiful Messianic passage. This is clear from verse 6 where God says:

> *It is too small a thing for you to be my servant*
> *to restore the tribes of Jacob*
> *and bring back those of Israel I have kept.*
> *I will also make you a light for the Gentiles*
> *that you may bring my salvation to the ends of the*
>   *earth.*

We have moved from the restricted function of the Servant to the broader one. And we have moved from a localized people to a worldwide church!

This is a Psalm about the restoration of Israel under Cyrus, yes. But it is, more than that, a foreshortened psalm of the gathering of the elect out of the captivity of sin. Christ came to set the captive free. To be in him is to be free indeed. And Christ is saying 'Come out' to men

> *from afar –*
> *some from the north, some from the west,*
> *some from the region of Sinim.*

All of this was in the mind of God before the earth's formation. And in his mind each one of his people existed. He had a purpose for each – to be his servant. Even to be his son!

> *Praise be to the God and Father of our Lord Jesus Christ, who has blessed us in the heavenly realms with every spiritual blessing in Christ. For he chose us in him before the creation of the world to be holy and blameless in his sight. In love he predestined us to be adopted as his sons (Ephesians 1:3–5a).*

Give Us More Space

[Isaiah 49:14–26]

Local congregations have many kinds of problems, but the best kind is the space problem. We rejoice to hear of the church that builds a new building only to find that by the time it is completed it is too small!

This is the problem that God promised to Zion. And he promises it to the church of Christ today. The promise was kept the day refugees from captivity returned to their home land and Jerusalem was rebuilt. It is being kept here and there today as men and women are coming to the Mountain of the Lord to hear the gospel message. It is happening in Africa where the demand for Bibles can scarcely be met. It is happening in South America where the largest Christian churches in the world flourish. As Christ continues to build his church it will happen more and more. And one day his people will stand in amazement to see the throngs from every tribe and nation and age gathered around the throne. Where did they all come from? we will ask. Who told them of Christ? Who nurtured them?

There are times when we, like Zion, feel forsaken. We feel that the Lord has forgotten us. Especially concerning the lack of response to the gospel do we become discouraged – pastors and all other Christians alike. We seem to be so few: in our church, our nation, our world.

Our Lord is aware of these times and feelings and he addresses himself to them. He encourages us by comparing himself to a mother and professing his love. In case we point to spreading child abuse he says,

> *Though she [mother] may forget you,*
> *I will not forget you!*

He encourages us by picturing a mother who is surrounded by her children, who wears them as a bride wears her ornaments. He points us to the day when, in all parts of the world, children will be added to our fellowship of worship. He reminds us, does he not, of the thousands in Korea who gather for sunrise prayer meetings. 'Give us more space,' they may say as they huddle on the floor. 'Who bore me these?' the Korean church may wonder, as the faithful gather daily to blend their voices in prayer.

And further, our Lord encourages us with the promise that

> *All mankind will know*
> *that I, the Lord, am your Saviour,*
> *your Redeemer, the Mighty One of Jacob.*

As our Saviour he will protect us against his and our enemies. And all mankind will bow before him.

> *Thank you, our God, for taking us seriously in our moments of despair and distress. Recall to our minds that we are not just a handful of people in an alien world. We are your people, your children, and one day we shall be crying out to you, 'Give us more space!'*
>
> *Remind us, too, that in the many rooms in heaven there will be space for all your elect.*

I Have Not Drawn Back

[Isaiah 50]

Because of their sins God's people were sold into captivity. They were unfaithful and disobedient servants, as we have been.

But, as we read in verses four to nine, the Servant Jesus was not disobedient. Isaiah has told us about him before. Here there are more words prophetic of him, strong words that come from his mouth – words of One leaning heavily on the Sovereign Lord.

Jesus was given by God an instructed tongue. 'No one ever spoke the way this man does' (John 7:46). His instructed tongue knew the word to sustain the weary, 'Come to me, all you who are weary and burdened, and I will give you rest' (Matthew 11:28).

He daily wakened to take early morning lessons from his teacher. 'The words I say to you are not just my own. Rather it is the Father, living in me, who is doing his work' (John 14:10).

He was not rebellious. He did not draw back. 'Not my will, but yours be done,' he prayed in the garden (Luke 22:42).

He accepted the abuse heaped upon him. He made no reply to Pilate, 'not even to a single charge' (Matthew 27:14).

Because the Sovereign Lord helped him, he was not disgraced. Calmly he faced his accusers. He set his face like a flint. 'He resolutely set out for Jerusalem,' (Luke

9:51) assured that he would not be put to shame. He did not draw back.

No one could really lay anything to his charge. 'Who is my accuser?' Isaiah has him say. The Sanhedrin found no evidence against him. Even Pilate said, 'I . . . have found no basis for your charges against him' (Luke 23:14).

He was, and is, the light of the world. All who put their trust in him will be in the light and will have life without end. 'I am the light of the world. Whoever follows me will never walk in darkness, but will have the light of life' (John 8:12).

Why should any fail to trust in the name of the Lord and to fear him? Why should any not obey the word of God's servant?

But some, said the prophet, *will* refuse to walk in the light, preferring to light fires of their own and to provide themselves with torches of their own devising. To these the Lord says,

> *Go, walk in the light of your fires*
> *and of the torches you have set ablaze.*
> *This is what you shall receive from my hands:*
> *You will lie down in torment.*

O Lord, we have no light of our own. We walk in the light of your Son who went all the way to Calvary for us, not drawing back. Help us. And may we never draw back!

The Rock from Which You Were Cut

[*Isaiah 51:1–16*]

C. S. Lewis, in his paper 'On the Reading of Old Books,' advises: 'It is a good rule, after reading a new book, never to allow yourself another new one till you have read an old one in between. If that is too much for you, you should at least read one old one to every three new ones.' Among others of his reasons he makes the point that if we restrict ourselves to the ideas of our own age we narrow our view and become trapped by the shortsightedness of contemporary thinking. We rob ourselves of the understanding of the sweep of the thought of men through the centuries.

God is saying something similar to that in Isaiah 51. He tells us to look back – to our roots, to the rock from which we were cut and the quarry from which we were hewn. We, along with Isaiah's contemporaries, are told to look back even to Abraham, our forebear in the faith.

The Jews were to look to Abraham not simply because there was greatness in him, although surely God made him to be a great man. Rather they were to look to him because God had given him a special place in history as the father of the faithful. It was important for them to remember this.

Spoken first to Israel, this call to look to the rock from which we were cut has an implication for the church today. We profit by looking to Abraham. We are encouraged to see that the promises to him are

promises to us and to see them being kept by
Abraham's God and ours. We are encouraged to sense
the unity of God's people from Abraham onwards even
to ourselves.

We are encouraged, too, as we look back to David
and to Paul. As we see their faith, their boldness, their
love, their devotion to God, we are taught lessons in
Christian living. And we are taught lessons in the
faithfulness of God to his people throughout history.

We would do well, also, to look to the men through
whom the gospel came to us in more recent centuries.
Would not God have us acquainted with Augustine and
Luther and Spurgeon? These men were raised up as
links in the chain that was forged with Abraham, a
chain to which God has been adding through the
centuries. We can better understand ourselves and our
faith as we look to them.

In Hebrews 12 God gives us one of the values of
looking back. These who went before us are a crowd of
witnesses to the faith of God who spur us on in the race
we are running. Wycliffe calls out, 'Be brave!' Machen
says to us, 'Keep the faith!'

But the rock from which we were cut was, ultimately,
God himself. We are his workmanship and we are made
in his image. And from the two human agents whom he
fashioned in Eden he has called forth a people whose
thousands stand forth for their Maker. As we look back
to our Creator we marvel. And only as we look to him do
we *live*!

Our faith is strengthened by God's promises to
comfort Zion and to bring her joy and gladness and the
sound of singing. Our faith is strengthened, too, as we
hear our Lord speak of how his justice will become a
light to the world. From our side of Calvary we look at

this fifth verse and know that God's righteousness has come, his salvation has been accomplished, and his gospel has begun to bring justice to the nations. We rejoice to hear our God say, 'My salvation will last forever, my righteousness will never fail.'

Sometimes we are afraid. But we fear only as we forget the Lord our Maker, or as we forget how he has been with his people. He has called us into a fellowship with his saints through the ages: one people united in him. Let us read our history. Let us remember the rock from which we have been cut.

The Goblet That Makes Men Stagger

[*Isaiah 51:17–23*]

God's wrath, poured out because of sin even upon his own children, is likened to wine that makes them stagger as they drain the dregs. The calamities that have come upon them have been a rebuke from their God. He has sent enemies to attack them and to take them captive.

As children of Adam we stagger, too, from the goblet of God's wrath. The ravages of sin upon this universe with its floods and blizzards and volcanoes are experienced by God's people along with the rest of mankind. Disease, disaster and death itself are enemies of Christians as well as their neighbors. Hate, greed, deceit and murder have their effect upon the righteous and ungodly alike. We stagger at the goblet.

Assyrian monuments show victors walking upon the backs of conquered foes. The enemies of God's people have perpetrated upon them degradation and disgrace throughout history. Whether literally or figuratively, they have ordered God's people to fall prostrate while they walked upon them in the streets.

But we need to rise in the midst of our stupor and listen to what our Sovereign God says. He will take the goblet from our hands and we will never drink again! He will put it in the hands of those who torment us. John speaks about the worshiper of the beast in these terms: 'He, too, will drink the wine of God's fury, which has been poured full strength into the cup of his wrath' (Revelation 14:10).

Isaiah's contemporaries took courage as they looked to the day when their enemies would be experiencing their due punishment from God. They looked beyond the captivity to the day when they themselves would be at peace.

But when we think about the goblet of God's wrath and about its being taken away not to be drunk again by his people, we need to think about Christ.

Look at Gethsemane. The Lord Jesus was awaiting his arrest. He prayed with full knowledge of what was before him and of the reason for his coming suffering and death. So heavy was his heart that he prayed that, if possible, the cup be taken from him. It was not possible. The penalty for sin had to be paid that God's chosen ones might not have to bear it. So the Saviour drank the cup. He drained the goblet to its dregs.

So it is that although the results of sin are all about us, although we feel their effects every day of our life, as do the children of Satan, God's wrath is not directed toward us. We have sinned as have all men. But our

Saviour has drunk the goblet and we will never have to drink it. Praise his holy name!

Your God Reigns

[*Isaiah 52:1-12*]

This is the story of the return of the Jews to their homeland and holy city. First Isaiah speaks to Jerusalem herself. He tells her that the heathen will not enter her again. She will shake off the dust of her degradation and rise to sit on her throne again in the garment of her splendor.

God's people had lived through Egyptian captivity. Many had been their enemies through the years. Now Assyria had oppressed her. And God's name had been constantly blasphemed. But the day will come when they will know his name. As he lays bare his holy arm in the sight of the nations, all will see his salvation.

The delight of the return is captured in a picture of messengers on the mountains, bearing good news. Even their feet, which symbolize their swiftness, are beautiful. They are beautiful because of the message they bring: 'Your God reigns.'

The message is peace, good tidings (literally *good news of good*) and salvation. The watchmen, hearing the news, lift up their voices and shout, 'Your God reigns!' Jerusalem, though now in ruins, bursts into songs of joy because the Lord has redeemed her and brought comfort to her people.

Yet a word of warning comes through to the religious leaders. As they leave Babylon with the vessels which are to be returned to God's temple from which they had been stolen, they are not to bring along anything that is unclean. No traces of idolatry or heathen worship are to be allowed to creep into the worship of Jehovah.

> *Depart, depart, go out from there!*
> *Touch no unclean thing!*

They are to be pure.

The departure of the Jews will not be in haste or in flight as it had been from Egypt. The Lord will be going before them, and behind, and will protect them. Cyrus, as God's agent, will secure their safety.

It is a beautiful picture. There is joy and delight. It is a true homecoming. A release. A victory. And it is a testimony to the world that the God of the Jews reigns, not only over his own special people but over all nations.

Fred S. Shepherd's hymn captures the victory of these words and brings out the Messianic overtones of this chapter.

> *Church of Christ, awake, awake!*
> *Thy God reigneth!*
> *Forward, then, fresh courage take:*
> *Thy God reigneth!*
> *Soon, descending from his throne,*
> *He shall claim thee for his own;*
> *Sin shall then be overthrown:*
> *Thy God reigneth, Thy God reigneth!*

The messengers on the mountain shout the gospel message. The watchmen take up the cry. And Jerusalem bursts into song. God has come to reign in the person of his Son who has brought peace and salvation to his people.

Join the chorus, O church of Christ, and shout the good tidings, 'Your God reigns!'

He Will Be Satisfied

[Isaiah 52:13–53:12]

Isaiah here presents the sufferings of the Saviour so graphically and poignantly that God's people through the years have turned to these lines repeatedly for meditation upon his passion. This was true of the writers of the Gospels, who quoted from it extensively when they recounted the experiences in the life of Christ which fulfilled these prophetic words. It is true today as we look back at prophecy and fulfilment together and marvel at the omniscience and love of the Father and of the Son.

Let us meditate upon that suffering. His appearance was so disfigured, 'beyond that of any man,' that many were appalled at him. His form was 'marred beyond human likeness'. He had no beauty or majesty that would make him attractive. There was nothing in his appearance that would cause men to desire him.

Rather, they despised and rejected him. He was 'a man of sorrows.' He was familiar with suffering. He was despised as a person men are loath to look at. He was held in low esteem.

He assumed the infirmities of his people and their

sorrows. He was stricken by God himself, smitten and
afflicted by him. He was pierced and crushed because
of men's sins. He bore the punishment, the wounds,
that men deserved. Indeed, the burden of men's sins
was the greatest burden he bore. This far exceeded the
physical pain. Because of it he experienced separation
from God. He experienced hell.

He was oppressed and afflicted, led as a lamb to be
butchered. So he was put to death – before he even
had a son to carry on his name. And he was buried
with wicked men.

Thus Isaiah portrays him; and so the gospel writers
portray him.

But, says Isaiah, 'he . . . will be satisfied!' This
suffering was not purposeless and ineffectual. 'By his
wounds we are healed.' He bore the sin of his people
and he made intercession for them. He did what he set
out to do. As he hung on the cross he said, 'It is
finished.' He did what was necessary according to the
righteous requirements of his Father. So he was
satisfied.

It is one thing to meditate upon the depths of his
suffering. It is something else to go beyond that, and
to dwell on the fact that it was for us he suffered and
died. How can we read these words of the prophet and
be the same?

*Lord Jesus, we are ashamed that we caused you to
suffer and that we have been so insensitive to your pain.
We are ashamed of our frequent coldness in the face of
your self-forgetting love.*

*But we find comfort in knowing that you are satisfied.
We are comforted that you do not consider your sor-
rowing and death in vain! Our salvation made it worth*

your while. We cannot understand it, but we say, Thank you.

Thank you. Thank you.

Do Not Hold Back

[Isaiah 54]

The students of William Carey's geography class sometimes saw their teacher weep as he pointed on the map to distant continents, islands and peoples. 'And these are pagans, pagans!' he would say.

On May 31, 1792 in Nottingham, England, Carey preached a sermon which has been called 'a burning bush of missionary revelation.' On the heels of this sermon came Carey's mission to India and the opening for Christ of that country which is today experiencing fresh fulfilment of Carey's expectation. Verses 2 and 3 of this chapter of Isaiah were the text from which he preached. They came from his mouth as a resounding plea that the gospel be proclaimed throughout the world. Carey was a disciple of John Eliot and Eliot's spirit was his. Eliot had said, 'Prayer and pains, through faith in Jesus Christ, will do anything.' Carey's message was, 'Expect great things from God. Attempt great things for God.'

Sometimes the church, resting in the beloved doctrines of God's sovereignty and of a gospel of grace alone, shudders at Carey's boldness. But his approach was not at variance with Reformed principles of evangelism. We quote him: 'We are sure that only those who are ordained to eternal life will believe, and that God alone can add to the church such as shall be saved. Nevertheless we cannot but observe with admiration that Paul, the great champion for the glorious doctrines of free and sovereign grace, was the most conspicuous for his personal zeal in the work of persuading men to be reconciled to God.'

The church today needs the message of Isaiah and Carey. The picture of the desolate woman bearing children, of her tent being enlarged, of her descendants dispossessing the nations, needs to be held up before the church as Isaiah and Carey held it up in their days. Christians need to see that the architect of the expansion of the kingdom is none else but our Maker and that not without reason is he called 'the God of all the earth.'

Both as a body and as individuals we need, as did Isaiah's Israel, the promises of God's unfailing love, of his covenant of peace that will not be removed, of protection against every weapon that is forged against us. With these promises there is no reason for us to be afraid. Resting upon them we will not fear the man next door who must be confronted with his need of God. We will not fear the forces that militate against the family and traditional values. We will not fear the tyranny that would rob men of their freedom to worship God.

Assured that our Maker is our husband, that the Holy One of Israel is our Redeemer, we must go ahead to enlarge our tent, to stretch our tent curtains wide, to lengthen our cords and strengthen our stakes. Confident that the Lord Almighty is God of all the earth we must not hold back in our efforts to proclaim his message to all. God is declaring here that we may expect great things from him. Let us ask ourselves, 'How much am I attempting for him?'

The Richest of Fare

[*Isaiah 55:1–7*]

How we enjoy going to an especially fine French restaurant and feasting on food prepared carefully and served attractively. But the cost! Most of us enjoy this sort of an outing a great deal more if we are guests of a generous host.

God, the great provider, holds out for our taking the richest of fare. He offers us wine and milk, symbols of the finest fruits of the land. He tells us to eat what is good.

But his dinner is free! His invitation is universal: to all the thirsty and hungry even if they be poor. What he offers is a feast obtainable without money or cost. No charge is made when the meal is finished. In fact, the meal is never finished!

Not that what he offers was obtained without cost; he paid for it with the cost of the life of his own Son. But we may have it without cost to us. 'For it is by grace you have been saved, through faith – and this not from yourselves, it is the gift of God – not by works, so that no one can boast' (Ephesians 2:8).

The water in Isaiah 55 is the water in Isaiah 12 where God brought his people to the wells of salvation. He offers this water freely. He *urges* the thirsty: 'Come . . . come . . . come . . . ' This richest of fare is for the spirit: it is a message. So he says: 'Listen . . . listen . . . eat . . . give ear . . . hear.'

The richest of fare is a message, yes, of salvation by grace, but it is truly the Lord himself. Notice these words:

> *Seek* the Lord *while he may be found;*
> *call on him while he is near.*

And as we feast on this richest of fare our souls will delight. Our souls will live! They will live eternally.

God causes us here to examine our priorities. It was the tenth commandment that Paul admits brought him to his knees before the Saviour: 'Thou shalt not covet.' What about us? Do we show more interest in gourmet food than in food for our souls? than in the Lord himself? Isaiah challenges us:

> *Why spend money on what is not bread,*
> *and your labour on what does not satisfy?*

We get up from the dinner table well satisfied and content. But in the morning we are hungry again. God's fare will satisfy us eternally. It is 'food that endures to eternal life, which the Son of Man will give you' (John 6:27).

'I am the bread of life,' Jesus said. 'He who comes to me will never go hungry, and he who believes in me will never be thirsty . . . Your forefathers ate the manna in the desert, yet they died . . . I am the living bread that came down from heaven. If a man eats of this bread, he will live for ever' (John 6:35 ff.).

Let the unbeliever forsake his ways and in his spiritual hunger turn to the Lord. Let the sinner come to God in poverty of soul, claiming the merits of the Saviour. God will have mercy on him and will spread before him the richest of fare.

As the Heavens Are Higher Than the Earth

[*Isaiah 55:6–13*]

God calls on the wicked to forsake his way and the evil man to forsake his thoughts. He calls on man to come to him for pardon, explaining why this is necessary:

> *For my thoughts are not your thoughts,*
> *neither are your ways my ways.*

My ways and thoughts, says the Lord, are higher than yours 'as the heavens are higher than the earth'.

Are we plagued with pride? In our intellectual arrogance do we look to ourselves rather than to our Maker? Let us place our ways beside the ways of God and see how they compare. Let us go out into his world and watch the gentle rain coming down upon the parched lawn and see the grass being refreshed practically before our eyes. Let us watch after a cool night while the water evaporates from the roadway with the heat of the morning sun. The beautiful cycle of nature that we see here was called by godless man *meaningless*

[185]

(Ecclesiastes 1:1 ff.). How blind is such a response! Instead, man's response should be worship of the Creator God whose ways are so beautifully conceived and so effective for his purpose.

Do we wonder at the slowness of God's work? Do we ask, 'Where is this "coming" he promised?' (2 Peter 3:4) Where is his healing? Do we allow doubt and unbelief to make us impatient that he tarries in bringing about what he has promised? Again we need to observe the cycle of nature; to appreciate God's plan and observe the stateliness of all he does, the majestic and unrushed deliberateness.

God's plan cannot be hurried, but neither can it be foiled. As we submit to it, as we accommodate our timing to his, even our will to his, we shall be at peace. We shall learn to rest in the surety of his higher ways and thoughts.

We shall go out again into his world and marvel:

> *You will go out in joy*
> *and be led forth in peace;*
> *the mountains and hills*
> *will burst into song before you,*
> *and all the trees of the field*
> *will clap their hands.*

We shall know that this is all for the glory of the One who brought it about, the One whose desires are always accomplished, who achieves the purpose for which he does all things. As Isaiah says:

> *This will be for the Lord's renown,*
> *for an everlasting sign,*
> *which will not be destroyed.*

What sign has God given that his will is going to be done? The cycle of nature is such a sign. And so is the progress – throughout the centuries and the world – of the gospel of his Son. His word will not return unto him void. He will accomplish in the hearts of men and in the nations of the earth what he purposes.

The evaporation of moisture from the earth assures us of the rain that will come and water the earth. The entrance of one soul into his kingdom assures us of the nations that will surround his heavenly throne.

We can *trust* him. Isn't it comforting as we recognize our own ignorance, inconsistency, short-sightedness, impatience, to be assured by his signs that his thoughts and ways are higher than ours?

A House of Prayer for All Nations

[Isaiah 56:1–8]

It has been observed by students of church growth that churches which experience the most phenomenal growth are generally those with a homogeneous constituency. We are in no position to refute this observation. But it must be pointed out that God's Holy Spirit is not limited in his power to draw men to the Saviour. And might it not be that God is pleased to receive greater glory through a small, struggling church that has wide open doors for those who are different: foreigners (people 'from away' as the old-time people of Maine refer to persons born outside their state), people with a different accent, a different dress code, or a different colored skin, those who have a handicap or are disadvantaged in some other way? In these churches particularly is fulfilled God's word through Isaiah,

> . . . *My house will be called*
> *a house of prayer for all nations.*

This is true in the church universal. God would have it true in the church at the corner of Second and Market Streets.

As foreigner and eunuch come to the temple of God to worship him, as they love his name and obey his commandments, they demonstrate that they are his indeed. He is the Lord of the whole universe and, when his people at last worship him in glory, men and women from every tribe and language will be there: the faithful in mainland China and the happy lepers in their colonies in Korea, singing their hymns of praise. They will be there. They, as well as we, are among the others Isaiah speaks of in verse eight,

> *I will gather still others to them*
> *besides those already gathered.*

The Lord Jesus said, 'I have other sheep that are not of this sheep pen. I must bring them also. They too will listen to my voice, and there shall be one flock and one shepherd' (John 10:16). Later he said, 'My prayer is not for them alone. I pray also for those who will believe in me through their message' (John 17:20). He has his own in all nations and he will gather them into his house of prayer.

And always it is by grace. There is nothing in the foreigner, who knows little of the faithfulness of the Covenant God through Israel's turbulent history, that can secure for him access to the temple of God. There is nothing in the eunuch to admit him into the presence of a God who required physical perfection in the sacrifices that were offered to him. There is nothing in you or me, once strangers to the covenant, sinful, blind – even dead! All men are the same before him. One needs his grace in salvation as much as another.

And the grace of God that brings salvation has appeared to men. Through God's Son, all men, whether they be respected members of society or whether they be outcasts in the eyes of the world, may come into God's house of prayer. They may commune with God!

Mute Dogs

[Isaiah 56:9–12]

In the Farnsworth Museum in Rockland, Maine, there hangs a painting by N. C. Wyeth of a blind father holding the hand of his blind wife who in turn holds their young son's hand. With calm trust wife and son follow the leading of this man unaware that a few feet before them drops a steep cliff. Below this work are engraved in brass the words, 'The Blind Leading the Blind.'

This is, to the believer, a picture of the father, who should be prophet, priest and king to his family, leading them to destruction because of his own lack of spiritual sight. It is a picture of the spiritual leader, whose eyes have not been opened by the Saviour's touch, leading God's people into sin and sorrow rather than on to the heavenly city. It is a tragic picture.

In the early part of Isaiah 56 we find encouragement and assurance for persons who might have some reason to believe that they would not be acceptable to the God of Jacob and welcome in his house of prayer. Here God turns to those who feel most secure: the shepherds of the flock and the watchmen of the people. He speaks to the pastors and ruling elders, the deacons, the Sunday School teachers and youth workers – and to the parents.

To these he does not give words of welcome into his house or an affirmation that their offering will be acceptable on his altar. Instead, he summons the beasts of the fields and the forest to come and devour them! Why? Because they are blind and content to be blind. They are ignorant and unwilling to learn. They are mute dogs. When there is danger to the flock of God they do not bark to scare away the enemy or to warn the sheep. They enjoy lying around – sleeping, dreaming. They are voracious dogs who never have enough to eat. They are shepherds who do not have understanding. They all go their own way, each seeking his own gain. They indulge themselves and then become even less rational, fooling themselves about reality and the inevitability of judgment.

God is calling upon the wild animals to destroy false teachers in his house who think they are secure in the fold. James says, 'Not many of you should presume to be teachers, my brothers, because you know that we who teach will be judged more strictly' (James 3:1). Isaiah along with James impresses upon us the awful responsibility of being in a place of leadership among the people of God.

Insidiously, errors creep into the church and the watchmen must be diligent. Paul told the church in Ephesus, 'I know that after I leave, savage wolves will come in among you and will not spare the flock . . . So be on your guard! Remember that for three years I never stopped warning each of you night and day with tears' (Acts 20:29–31). What pastor among us can claim such diligence over his flock?

God has given us a model of shepherding. He describes himself as our shepherd in the twenty-third Psalm. Jesus calls himself the Good Shepherd, too, in John 10, the shepherd who gives his life for his sheep. This example is for all who 'presume to be teachers.'

When did your pastor last bark? Or your Sunday School teacher? When did *you* last bark? Pray that the sleeping dogs may be wakened, that they may be given eyes to see, hearts of compassion and understanding, and voices to sound the alarm.

Or else pray that God may call upon the beasts of the field to drive them from the church where they are failing the sheep and the little lambs!

No One Ponders It in His Heart

[*Isaiah 57:1–13*]

Why do the good die young? How often this is asked. Here God addresses himself to this question:

> *Devout men are taken away,*
> *and no one understands*

> *that the righteous are taken away*
> *to be spared from evil.*
> *Those who walk uprightly*
> *enter into peace;*
> *they find rest as they lie in death.*

How beautifully reassuring are these words!

For a moment, however, God turns his attention from these persons to those who are rebels, liars, idolators. They, he says, will suffer the just deserts of their ungodliness. God will expose their righteousness (which is not righteousness); he will expose their works (which are evil and not good works). Such men will cry out to their gods but will not be heard. Their righteousness and works will not benefit them. There is no peace or rest promised for them. Their future is bleak.

From such a future the truly righteous will be spared. God says,

> *The man who makes me his refuge*
> *will inherit the land*
> *and possess my holy mountain.*

It will be far better for them in death than to live in a world which is reaping the judgment of men who have prostituted themselves with man-made gods, forsaking their husband and Maker.

Why, indeed, do we question God when we see his people die? When we grieve at the *untimely* (was it not God's time?) death of a child, why do we shake our heads and doubt God's love? God has given us this word from Isaiah to help us to understand his ways that are higher than our ways. Death can be gracious. In our bereavement let us remember this and give thanks that our loved one is not experiencing the upheaval and unrest of this 'present evil world' but is finding rest as he lies in death.

With the fuller revelation of God's truth that comes with the New Testament, the nature of the Christian experience after death is expanded upon. Paul spoke of death as being 'with the Lord, which is far better' (Philippians 1:23). John spoke of becoming like Christ when we shall see him as he is. In the New Jerusalem, John tells us, as Isaiah also does, that there will be no night, no tears. The whole picture, which we can construct as we read the New Testament alongside the Old, is one of peace and rest for the child of God.

Help us to ponder this in our hearts, O Lord. Comfort us by this thought. Help us, too, to be bold to tell salvation's story so that men may pass from death unto life.

Peace, Peace

[*Isaiah 57:14–21*]

As this is written the sea outside our window is calm and blue. Yesterday it tossed angrily, hurling seaweed and debris from its muddy brown waves on to the shore. It brought home the picture of the wicked as God presents him through Isaiah:

The wicked are like the tossing sea
which cannot rest,
whose waves cast up mire and mud.

> *There is no peace, says my God,*
> *for the wicked.*

But the man who is contrite and lowly in spirit is like today's peaceful sea – beautiful, controlled. God says first:

> *I was enraged by his sinful greed;*
> *I punished him, and hid my face in anger.*

But he also says, 'I will not accuse forever . . . I will heal him.' To these, far and near, he promises peace and healing.

Indeed, God *has* healed his people, having placed the punishment due them upon his own Son.

As we read the injunction in verse 14 to prepare the road and remove the obstacles, we think again of John the Baptist making ready a highway in the desert for the approach of God's Son. The High and Lofty One promises his presence with the lowly in spirit. And John welcomed the One who had inhabited the heavenlies when he came to live among the men he had created.

One day this One was in a boat that tossed on the Sea of Galilee. His disciples were terrified at the high waves that suddenly began to sweep over the boat. They woke the Lord from slumber in the stern, and he stood up, looking out at the maelstrom. 'Quiet!' he said, 'Be still!' (Mark 4:39). Or, as the Authorized Version translates it, 'Peace, be still.' The wind died down and the sea became completely calm.

Sometimes our faith is so little and we tremble. We say, 'Teacher, don't you care if we drown?' (Mark 4:38). Why do we forget that in life's most tumultuous times we may have the peace of the Christ who is in the boat with us?

The peace and rest promised to the devout and righteous man at death has a counterpart here on earth. Storms come. There is sorrow, illness, bereavement. But within the soul there is peace, because the Prince of Peace himself dwells within the hearts of his people.

You Do as You Please

[*Isaiah 58*]

All through the book of Isaiah we see that God wants his people to worship him. Among other provisions he has made for worship are the Sabbath Day, set aside especially for man's devotion to God, and the fast, a period of particular devotion characterized by abstinence and by prayer, especially at the time of some particular traumatic experience. These two means for worship which God has provided are highlighted in Isaiah 58.

But how carefully he points out that the Sabbath and the fast are not, as bare activities, real worship. We can go through the rituals of the Sabbath and the fast and appear to our neighbors to be God's people and yet go unnoticed by God. Isaiah writes:

> *For day after day they seek me out;*
> *they seem eager to know my ways,*
> *as if they were a nation that does what is right*
> *and has not forsaken the commands of its God.*

They ask me for just decisions
and seem eager for God to come near them.

In fact, they may fool a lot of people. They certainly appear to be fooling themselves. But they are not fooling God.

We read in 1 Samuel 16:7, ' . . . The Lord does not look at the things man looks at. Man looks at the outward appearance, but the Lord looks at the heart.' Our God looks beyond the act of worshiping into the heart of the worshiper.

As Jesus said to the woman at the well, 'God is a Spirit, and his worshipers must worship in spirit and in truth.' His worshipers are to be singleminded. He asks for conformity to his will in men's lives so that everything we do harmonizes with every other thing. We are to be totally bent upon obeying and serving the God we worship.

As we seek to please God by fasting and keeping his day holy we are to seek to please him at the office, in the shop, at home, at the swimming pool. To please him is to right social wrongs, to release from oppression men who are unjustly treated, to share our food with the hungry, and to provide the poor wanderers with shelter and clothing. To please him is to love, to forgive, to be patient, to be humble.

Some of Isaiah's compatriots were not seeking to please God in this way. They were doing as they pleased. The man whose fast is a sham was condemned in verse 3 for doing as he pleases. God tells his true worshiper to keep from doing *as he pleases*: 'If you keep . . . from doing *as you please* on my holy day . . . and if you honor it by . . . not doing *as you please*, then you will find your joy in the Lord' (v. 13). Men's dulness causes God to repeat this phrase several times.

But in God's divine irony, if we submit ourselves to him and commit ourselves to doing what *he* pleases in every department of our lives, we shall discover a strange thing: we shall be pleased to do what pleases him. As we grow in our knowledge of Christ and are more and more conformed to his image, what God pleases and what we please will be one.

> *Our Father, help us so to grow. Transform our thinking and our feeling and our living so that all of our life may be a symphony with the theme of praise to you. We want to be called Repairer of Broken Walls. We want to ride on the heights of the land.*

The Arm of the Lord – Not Too Short to Save

[*Isaiah 59*]

Lady Macbeth, who had prided herself on her manly courage, is walking in her sleep. She rubs her hands, vainly seeking to rid them of the blood of her murders. 'Yet here's a spot,' she moans. 'Out, damned spot! out, I say! . . . Here's the smell of the blood still: all the perfumes of Arabia will not sweeten this little hand.' For centuries men have felt the poignancy of this scene. Sin! Guilt! Conscience! All are compressed in this scene of a pitiable woman who seeks in vain to rid herself of the stains of blood on her hands and soul.

Shakespeare used with reference to Lady Macbeth

the same figure Isaiah had used nearly 2,400 years before with reference to Israel:

> *For your hands are stained with blood,*
> *Your fingers with guilt.*
> *Your lips have spoken lies,*
> *And your tongue mutters wicked things.*

On and on he goes, describing the sin of man in a pile-up of terms that reminds us also of the early chapters of Romans!

Isaiah had begun by stating very clearly that God's arm is not so short that it cannot save. He is able to save. His ear is not so dull that it cannot hear. He is sensitive to the needs of man and has the means to meet them. God is neither impotent, nor ignorant, nor unfeeling.

But there is a barrier! God is holy. And man's sin has made a separation between him and his Creator. Man's sin has hidden God's face from him so that the communication is broken. The barrier that man raises up shuts out his cries from God.

So it is, the prophet goes on to say, that man looks for light and brightness but finds himself walking in deep shadows. He is like a blind man who gropes along the wall, feeling his way.

What is man to do? He is to repent of the sin that defiles his hands with blood and separates him from God. Isaiah even gives the words to use:

> . . . *Our offences are many in your sight,*
> *and our sins testify against us.*
> *Our offences are ever with us.*
> *and we acknowledge our iniquities.*

David sinned. He tells about it in Psalm 51 and about his repentance before his God. He admits that he knows his transgressions, that his sin is always before him. He recognizes that it is before God he has sinned. He says, 'Save me from bloodguiltiness, O God, the God who saves me.' David was guilty of the same sin before God as was Lady Macbeth. But David knew God and knew that as he confessed his sin the barrier between himself and the Holy God would be done away. He knew that by the sacrifice of the Saviour to come he could be clean and could find joy and gladness in reunion with his Father.

In his justice God must repay according to what men have done. But in his grace he has made a covenant with his elect. He says, 'My Spirit, who is on you, and my words that I have put in your mouth will not depart from your mouth, or from the mouths of your children, or from the mouths of their descendants from this time on and forever.'

O our God, we acknowledge our sin to you. Thank you for dealing with it on Calvary's cross. Thank you for your Spirit who has shown us our sin and enabled us to confess it and bow before you. Thank you that your arm is not too short to reach those who are far away from you.

Your Heart Will Throb

[*Isaiah 60*]

We cannot read too often of the New Jerusalem where there will be no need of sun or moon for light, because God will be the everlasting light. Isaiah glimpses this in verses 19 and 20. Beautifully he blends the promises of God for his ancient people: holding out the hope for their near future, for the days of the Messiah, and for the everlasting kingdom.

God will wipe away all tears, as we have noticed before. The days of sorrow will come to an end.

As we look about us we see men and women assembling and coming to us, the church of Christ. The angels of heaven rejoice over one sinner who repents. And our hearts throb and swell with joy as persons we have seen changing and blossoming confess Christ in our midst. These are the silver and gold and incense that most honor the Lord God. The thousands who proclaim his truth could vouch for the tens of thousands God is bringing to himself.

Sometimes our hearts nearly break with heaviness at the encroaching pollution, not only of the physical universe but of society. The increase in disrespect for human life weighs upon us heavily. Indeed,

> . . . *darkness covers the earth*
> *and thick darkness is over the peoples.*

But Isaiah arouses us: 'Arise, shine, for your light has come.' This is the cry we need to hear. The Light of the World has come and if our hearts have been touched by his glory they should throb and swell with joy now. You will be radiant, Isaiah says, as you see the Light shining forth and drawing men to himself. We will be radiant inasmuch as we are reflecting his light. We are moons, reflectors of the sun. As we reflect him it will be said of us, too, 'You are the light of the world' (Matthew 5:14).

[200]

The two disciples on the road to Emmaus were blind to the identity of the resurrected Jesus as he walked and talked with them. After he had gone and their eyes were opened they said, 'Were not our hearts burning within us while he talked with us on the road and opened the Scriptures to us?' (Luke 24:32).

Our hearts should burn! They should throb and swell with joy. How can we be cold in the presence of the Saviour? How can we remain unmoved as we see men turning from darkness to the Light that has come into the world? How can we help reflecting him? Our light has come. Let us shine!

Garments of Salvation

[Isaiah 61]

Clarence Duff, who labored in the gospel for many years in Ethiopia, used to enjoy telling about an interesting marriage custom in that country. The groom traditionally provided the wedding gown for his bride. And it was always a sparkling white cotton muslin gown. What an apt parallel to that which the divine Bridegroom does for his bride the church! Men and women come to him in their need, even in their filthy rags and nakedness. He clothes them with the garment of salvation, the robe of his own righteousness, as he takes them unto himself to be his own.

Jesus went into the synagogue on a particular Sabbath day. In Luke 4:16 ff. we pick up the account:

'He stood up to read. The scroll of the prophet Isaiah was handed to him. Unrolling it, he found the place where it is written:

> *The Spirit of the Lord is on me,*
> *because he has anointed me*
> *to preach good news to the poor.*
> *He has sent me to proclaim freedom for*
>   *the prisoners*
> *and recovery of sight for the blind,*
> *to release the oppressed,*
> *to proclaim the year of the Lord's favor.'*

As the Saviour sat down after reading the scroll he said, 'Today this scripture is fulfilled in your hearing.'

There are many who are poor in spirit. He preaches good news to them. So many are broken-hearted over their sins. He binds them up. So many are in captivity to the Evil One. He proclaims freedom to them. So many are blind to God's truth. He gives them sight. There are so many who mourn over their fragmented lives. He comforts them.

Today there is an awakening awareness among conservative Christians of the imperative need to minister to the physical needs of people as well as to the spiritual: to feed and clothe the poor, to bring healing to the sick, to visit the prisoner. These very verses in Isaiah have been used to underscore the need of such ministries. The whole gospel to the whole person is the note that is being struck. And surely the Lord is pleased with this balanced ministry.

In Christ himself we see the broad, balanced application of love in action embracing the physical needs of men whose lives he touched. With his miraculous powers he was able in a very special way to give sight to the physically blind and even to raise the dead. His soul of compassion reached out and responded to those whose lives were saddened by disease and disability.

However, in Isaiah here as well as in the words of Jesus in the beatitudes recorded in Matthew 5:3–10, the emphasis is upon the spiritual needs of men. And unless we see this emphasis we miss the deep truths God is addressing to us. Jesus ministered to the needs of the bodies of men but he also clothed the nakedness of their souls. He provided them with a garment to replace the filthy rags which were all they had to wear as they stood before their Maker, giving them a garment of his own righteousness. He gave his bride a garment of salvation.

This is why we may delight greatly in the Lord and why our souls may rejoice in our Saviour. We were in need and he made us just and right in our Father's sight. What security, to be clothed upon by Christ and to know that as God looks at us he sees the righteousness of his sinless Son!

All that Paul could claim – and he could claim much that would make a Jew proud – he counted rubbish. His sole desire was that he might, as he puts it with reference to himself, 'gain Christ and be found in him, not having a righteousness of my own that comes from the law, but that which is through faith in Christ – the righteousness that comes from God and is by faith' (Philippians 3:9).

And this garment of salvation has been given to us to cover our nakedness.

An additional word needs to be said. As the Bride of Christ we are indeed clothed with his perfect righteousness. No lesser robe could equip us to stand before our holy God. By faith alone is this garment received. But we must be jealous about righteousness more and more in our own walk. This comes about, thank God, as the fruit of the Spirit is developed in our own life. And this growing holiness is the mark of a maturing Christian life.

A New Name – Hephzibah

[Isaiah 62]

The righteousness of Zion will shine out like the dawn, we read here. We sometimes stand at daybreak and watch through squinting eyes as the grey sky begins to light up with pink and orange. We wait for the first sliver of sun to gleam on the Atlantic Ocean. And soon the whole red ball rides the horizon. As we recall Isaiah's comparison of the righteousness of Zion to the glory of the dawn, our sunrise trysts have special meaning. The Bride in all her glory is like the morning sky transformed by the rising sun.

In Malachi 4:2 we read, 'For you who revere my name, the sun of righteousness will rise with healing in its wings.' Traditionally God here has been considered to be referring to the coming of Christ, appearing as the rising of the sun. The Bride's blush of joy is a response to his coming.

In Isaiah 54 the poet had developed the figure of marriage to illumine our concept of the relationship of the chosen people to their God. Cast aside for a moment, Israel was renewed in her relationship to her Maker, her husband, with the promise of everlasting love.

Chapter 61 centered more on the wedding gown which was the garment of salvation and a robe of righteousness given the Bride by the Bridegroom. The jewels of her adorning in that chapter are reminiscent of Isaiah 49:18 where we read about the sons whom the bride will wear like ornaments.

Here in chapter 62 the theme of marriage is further developed. Zion, all glorious in her righteousness like the dawn, is to be called by a new name. No longer will she be called Deserted. Now her name will be Hephzibah, which means *My delight is in her*. So Isaiah says:

> *As a bridegroom rejoices over his bride,*
> *so will your God rejoice over you.*

Her land will have a new name, too. Instead of being called Desolate, it will be called Beulah, which means *Married*. Some Christians are uncomfortable with the gospel song, 'Beulah Land,' fearing that its imagery smacks too much of a hedonistic Moslem paradise. But God himself uses the term 'Beulah' to highlight the joy of a saving relationship with Christ. And as he uses it he shows the high regard with which he holds marriage! This is the land where the Bride lives with her husband.

God will guard the city where the Bride is to live. He has posted watchmen on her walls and they will call upon the Lord day and night, giving him

> *no rest till he establishes Jerusalem*
> *and makes her the praise of the earth.*

The importunity of the watchmen on the walls will be vindicated. The Lord tells them to say to the daughter of Zion, 'See, your Saviour comes!' And with the coming of the Saviour the Bride rejoices.

Still other names are given the Bride and her land:

> *They will be called the Holy People,*
> *The Redeemed of the Lord;*
> *And you will be called Sought After,*
> *The City No Longer Deserted.*

Thank you, our Saviour, for the new names you have given us. They help us to comprehend a little more the reality of your love for us.

Striding Forth in the Greatness of His Strength

[Isaiah 63]

The Conqueror, robed in splendor, strides forward in the greatness of his strength, having come from vanquishing the enemy, Edom. His garments are made deep red from the blood of nations he has trampled underfoot. He says, 'It is I, speaking in righteousness, mighty to save . . .'

Isaiah next directs his praise to this Conqueror:

> *I will tell of the kindnesses of the Lord,*
> *the deeds for which he is to be praised,*
> *according to all the Lord has done for us.*

The prophet reviews the history of Israel and sees how the Lord chose this people to be his own. How he redeemed them and carried them in his love and mercy. How he brought them through the Red Sea. How he set his Spirit among them. How he saved them.

Verse 9 is a high point:

> *In all their distress, he, too, was distressed,*
> *and the angel of his presence saved them.*

This same God who strode forward in the greatness of his strength is the one who sees and listens when his people receive hurt. He feels with them in the deepest periods of their depression. He shares their burdens and saves them by his very presence.

Isaiah pleads with God to remember his people now as he did in the past, not letting them wander from his ways. Enemies are trampling down God's sanctuary. Isaiah cries to him to return for the sake of his people.

He asks God, 'Where are your zeal and your might?' You who trampled the nations as grapes in a winepress, where is your power?

From our vantage point we see his zeal and might demonstrated. We see Israel returned from bondage and Jerusalem rebuilt. We see Christ striding forth in the greatness of his strength, having trodden the winepress alone and stained his clothing with the blood of the arch-enemy, Satan.

But is not this Conqueror, clothed with strength, a far cry from the meek Jesus on the tree, the Jesus whose garments were stained with his own blood shed for his people? Did not the meek Jesus, even as the enemy struck his heel, display only dignity, submission to the will of the Father and love for his own? Was there really this note of anger at Calvary?

Surely there was! Behind the scenes, in the realm of eternal transactions, certainly there was anger! There was holy wrath and vengeance as the Son of God was victoriously treading down the head of the serpent.

We look ahead to another scene, when our Lord will come again. He will come in love for his people, returning for the sake of his servants to protect them finally and to put to rout permanently those enemies of his loved ones who would snuff them out. This is the day of which John wrote, 'He is dressed in a robe dipped in blood, and his name is the Word of God' (Revelation 19:13).

Oh, That You Would Come Down

[*Isaiah 64*]

Isaiah continues to pray on behalf of the people. He has gathered them and us in his arms, and looking up to God he prays.

One theme, picked up in chapter 63, is prominent in his prayer:

> *Oh, that you would rend the heavens and*
> * come down*
> *that the mountains would tremble before you!*
> *. . . Come down to make your name known to*
> * your enemies.*
> *. . . For when you did awesome things that we did*
> * not expect*
> *you came down, and the mountains trembled*
> * before you.*

O Lord, he is saying, reveal yourself. Let us be aware in some new spectacular way of your existence and your power *today*. Perform some such mighty act as you did at the Red Sea. Let all the world know who you are.

Isaiah confesses that Israel has sinned:

> *All of us have become like one who is unclean;*
> *and all our righteous acts are like filthy rags.*

Our sins are as a wind which sweeps us away; we are spineless individuals with no more resistance than a shriveled leaf.

We deserve your anger, O Lord. It is no wonder you have hidden your face from us. But, O Lord, we are pots that you have made with your own hand. We are yours. Please, do not be angry beyond measure. Do not remember our sins for ever. Oh, that you would come down!

Isaiah looks at Jerusalem, where Israel's forefathers had worshiped God. In prospect he sees her lying in ashes. He sees all that Israel had treasured gone. The sins of her people and her turning from God have brought just punishment.

Did he see, too, in the faint future, another temple on the same site? Did he see the complete demolishing of that temple in 70 A.D.? Did he see his Israel, who had committed the arch sin of rejecting the King whom God had sent, now scattered and dissolved as a nation?

Isaiah looks through the sin-clouded atmosphere to heaven and pleads with God. You have punished us as we deserve. We confess our sin. Now, have you not done enough?

> *After all this, O Lord, will you hold yourself*
> *   back?*
> *Will you keep silent and punish us beyond*
> *   measure?*

God *has* come down. He has looked upon his people. He has not held himself back. He has not kept silent. Supremely, he has come down in the person of his Son. He has spoken to us through his Word. He looked upon us and saw our need. He gave himself to us freely in Christ, not holding back. Our sins had blown us away as a shrivelled leaf and the punishment we deserved at his hand has been borne by the Sinless One.

'How then can we be saved?' The question asked by Isaiah is one that needs to be asked today. And the answer is the same now as it was then. It is the answer that Paul gave to the Philippian jailer who asked, 'What must I do to be saved?' The answer is simply this, 'Believe in the Lord Jesus, and you will be saved – you and your household' (Acts 16:30, 31). God came down that this might be accomplished.

'Here Am I'

[*Isaiah 65:1–16*]

One time, when our children were younger, they spent the night in a tent on Little Island, just off shore directly opposite home. During the night a violent storm arose. Daddy, in the earliest dawn, rowed our little boat to the island to check on things.

As he approached the tent he heard a little voice say, 'I knew he'd come.' He *had* come, though they had not called.

What a feeble illustration! But perhaps it helps us

who are servants and children to see how we should rejoice and sing out in the joy of our hearts! Thank you, O Lord, for coming and saying, though we did not seek you, 'Here am I.'

Isaiah had prayed in chapter 64 that God would reveal himself. Here God answers: I have revealed myself. In fact, though the nation did not call upon my name, though they continually provoked me to my very face, though they practised heathen rites which caused them to be like smoke in my nostrils, I held out my hands to them. I said, 'Here am I, here am I.'

The Lord speaks to men in two ways. To those who forsake him and do not answer when he calls – who do not even listen – God answers with a sword. But there are others he does not destroy. They will be as juice squeezed from a cluster of grapes that had seemed to be dry. They are the righteous remnant. They are his servants. And they will live in Sharon and the Valley of Achor with their flocks and herds. For they sought him.

So it was. So it is. And so it will be. God's word speaks in two ways. This is why in Isaiah we have side by side the promises of future blessing and the threat of future judgment. There is a division among men.

There is a division even in the visible church today, just as there was in Israel. Now God addresses his servants. Now he addresses those who forsake him. He says to the latter,

> *My servants will eat,*
> *but you will go hungry;*
> *My servants will drink,*
> *but you will go thirsty;*
> *My servants will rejoice,*
> *but you will be put to shame.*

> *My servants will sing*
> *out of the joy of their hearts,*
> *but you will cry out*
> *from anguish of heart*
> *and wail in brokenness of spirit.*

This time has not yet come in its fulness, but it is sure. The Lord who revealed himself will perform it.

And we who are his servants, though we so ill deserve his favor, may rest in his promises that, should we go to the ends of the earth, we will hear a still, small voice through the night and storm saying, 'Here am I.' And we will say, 'We knew you would come, Lord.'

New Heavens and a New Earth

[Isaiah 65:17-25]

God continues to answer the questions the prophet asked in Isaiah 64:12:

> *After all this, O Lord, will you hold yourself*
> *   back?*
> *Will you keep silence and punish us beyond*
> *   measure?*

He speaks to Jerusalem, the city of the eighth century B.C. He had told her in Isaiah 64:11 (using again the prophetic past tense which considers an action completed because its accomplishment is so sure) that her temple, holy and glorious, would one day lie in ashes.

Now he reveals events beyond that time: Jerusalem will be rebuilt! Her walls will no longer re-echo with the sounds of crying. The times of captivity will be over and the Jews will again enjoy their own land.

But he is speaking, too, to Jerusalem the people. He is speaking to the faithful remnant, the Jerusalem which is God's servant, the chosen race through whom he will send his Son and to whom will be added people from all the world to sing his praises! He is speaking to the church.

To the church he is promising new heavens and a new earth. The church is the Bride that John tells about: 'I saw the Holy City, the new Jerusalem, coming down out of heaven from God, prepared as a bride beautifully dressed for her husband' (Revelation 21:2). In the Holy City the sorrows of this present earth will not be remembered. The pollution of this world as we know it will be unknown in this new earth. Heaven and earth will be one. It will be a place of delight. Life will not be cut short. Men will build houses and plant vineyards and will be able to enjoy them forever.

We are naturally curious about our eternal state. Many Christians see in this passage God's provision for the man he made in his own image to continue to be a creator even in the eternal kingdom. The church has been long accustomed to accepting music as an appropriate activity in heaven. From this passage we may add to music the building arts and horticulture. These avenues of praise are symbolic of others. God's praise will be reflected in all the fruit of man's labor. Man himself will long enjoy and find satisfaction in using the gifts God has given him. And whatever man does he will do for the glory of God.

God's blessing will be there – and his presence! There will be direct communication between God and his people. As in Eden? Even better, because there will be no possibility of falling.

And Jesus will be there – glorified! This is what he meant when he said, 'In my Father's house are many rooms; if it were not so I would have told you. I am going there to prepare a place for you. And if I go and prepare a place for you, I will come back and take you to be with me that you also may be where I am' (John 14:2 and 3).

But dust will be the serpent's food, just as God told him in the garden of Eden, 'You will eat dust' (Genesis 3:14). In that day, John tells us in Revelation, not only will the serpent's head be crushed but he will be utterly subdued. Only with his permanent, complete subjection will it be possible for heaven to be heaven. Only then will we be able to be completely glad and to rejoice for ever in the Jerusalem that God will create!

Even today in the fellowship of God's people we are experiencing a foretaste of heaven. But still sin lingers and mars that fellowship. Thank you, our God, for the hope Isaiah gives us in this picture of life in the new heavens and the new earth.

A Country Born in a Day

[*Isaiah 66:1–13*]

God speaks of men who have gone through the motions of worshiping him while they have been all the while choosing their own life-style. God says of them:

> ... *when I called, no one answered,*
> *when I spoke, no one listened.*

These have done evil and have displeased God. Their worship does not reach him. They will be put to shame.

But there will be those who listen. There will be those who tremble at his Word, who in humility and contrition recognize that God has spoken. These will receive God's peace coming with life-giving blessing like a flooding stream. They will be comforted by God as a child is comforted by his mother who nourishes him in her arms and dandles him on her knees. Note that the word *comfort* appears three times in verse 13!

These are Zion's children. And to Zion God makes the promise: she will bring forth children scarcely before labor has begun. This will be a sudden, surprising thing – 'a country born in a day.' God will not close up the womb when he brings to delivery. His promise is sure!

On one particular Pentecost a handful of believers that formed the young church was blessed by the outpouring of God's Holy Spirit. Peter preached. 'Those who accepted his message were baptized, and about three thousand were added to their number that day' (Acts 2:41). A country born in a day!

At the Protestant Reformation men emerged from medieval ignorance and dead formality to a zeal and power that could not be restrained by courts and councils. A country born in a day!

We think of revivals: of America called to her knees by Whitefield and his God, of England called to her knees by Spurgeon and his God! Countries born in a day!

[215]

And we think of the whole wide world full of nations who have been receiving the message of salvation through God's servants and experiencing the work of his Holy Spirit in a signal fashion – the early work and now the more recent work! We think of India. These, too, are countries born in a day.

But over and above all we think of the return of the Lord Jesus. Men and women and boys and girls from each of these times and places, and many more besides, will be all together in the presence of the Lord. From every tribe and nation they will be brought in ultimate fulfilment of Isaiah's prophecy.

Young people used to sing a gospel song that looked forward to this day with anticipation:

> *When we all get to heaven,*
> *What a day of rejoicing that will be;*
> *When we all see Jesus,*
> *We'll sing and shout the victory!*

Surely there will be no day like that day. A country will be born that day which will be like none other!

All Mankind . . . Will Bow Down

[*Isaiah 66:12–24*]

Isaiah is a strong book from a pastor's great heart. The prophet cannot put down his pen without once more reminding men that

> *with fire and with his sword*
> *the Lord will execute judgment upon all men,*
> *and many will be those slain by the Lord.*

Isaiah is a book of warning to those who will not bow the knee before the Creator and Redeemer.

For, really, Isaiah's prophecy is just this – a book about bowing down, about worship. In it God takes us into the starry night and reminds us of our smallness before him, so that we bend our knee on the dewy grass. He takes us to the throne of the Thrice-Holy One, just as he took Isaiah there.

God strips us of pride and superficiality and teaches us that true worship does not pertain to mere externals. It is of the heart. It is joy. And when we find our joy in him he causes us to ride on the heights of the land.

One day, through all the earth God's King will reign in glory. The earth will be filled with the knowledge of the Lord as the waters cover the sea. As we read in verse 20 of this chapter, brothers from all nations will be brought to God in the new Jerusalem, 'as an offering to the Lord.' You and I, perhaps in lands undreamed of by Isaiah, offer ourselves a living sacrifice before God. We are cleansed, as the vessels in which the Israelites brought grain offerings to the temple were cleansed. And we serve in the presence of the Lord.

In one sense, King Immanuel has already come to us. And from him we, like the woman of Samaria, have learned about worship. He has said to us, 'God is a Spirit, and his worshipers must worship in spirit and in truth' (John 4:24).

The Word of God is full of truth: it is *all* truth. And we need to be saturated in that pure truth to be able to worship the God of truth. But truth is sterile if it addresses only the intellect. The Word of God speaks not only to the intellect but to the spirit so that our worship may be spiritual.

Poetry, understood adequately, is a vehicle for communicating to the spirit. And Isaiah, the poet-prophet, called forth images that penetrate to our hearts. He used language that sings within us, reaching where prose can scarcely penetrate. Let us not be afraid to say it: Isaiah stirs our emotions.

To be convinced of this, turn to Isaiah 53. Much of the truth of this chapter could be expressed as history, theology – even psychology and pathology. But Isaiah couched these facts about the suffering Saviour in God-breathed poetic form, communicating not only divine truth to our minds but the love and condescension of God to our spirits. And only as we are *moved* by what God did for *us*, can we worship him.

Let the Christian stress truth for all he is worth. But let him not understress the spirit. Let the Bible be for him, not only God speaking to his mind, but also God speaking to his heart. Let the Christian be, not as the devils who believe in their minds and tremble, but as Thomas who finally fell to the ground in worship before the resurrected Jesus and said, 'My Lord and my God!' (John 20:28).

To fail to involve emotion in our worship, and indeed in all our life, is to starve the spirit. And atrophy of spirit is death indeed. The Gospel according to Isaiah, read humbly, honestly, devotionally, is an antidote for this crippling disease, this death.

Let us who have drunk of the wells of salvation read Isaiah again and again, and learn from him to worship the Lord in spirit and in truth. Such worship will make our hearts and the heart of God to rejoice as we join all redeemed mankind now and through eternity in bowing down in humility before him in the new heavens and the new earth!

'Then all the people said "Amen" and "Praise the Lord"' (1 Chronicles 16:36).